One Man's Journey

In Search of Freedom

OBERT C. TANNER

The Humanities Center at the University of Utah

One Man's Journey

In Search of Freedom

OBERT C. TANNER

The Humanities Center at the
University of Utah

ISBN 0-87480-445-0

First printing: September 1994

Frontispiece: Portrait of O. C. Tanner by Busath Photography,
Gateway Studios

Editorial management by Heather Bennett
Interior design and typography by Kristin Bernhisel-Osborn
Jacket design and photo layout by Bailey-Montague & Associates

Manufactured in the United States of America

Dedicated to companions on the journey,

Grace, my wife,

and

Annie, my mother.

CONTENTS

. . .

FOREWORD

...

The life story of Obert C. Tanner is one of multiple interests and achievements that set him apart as a very remarkable person. It is the tale of his struggle in humble and impoverished circumstances during his childhood and youthful years and, eventually, of his overwhelming success in many fields—as a scholar, as an industrialist, as a philanthropist, and as a statesman. Most particularly, the story reveals Obert Tanner as a humanitarian, a devoted family man, and a loyal friend.

What makes it fascinating reading is the author's desire and willingness to reveal his ambitions, his priorities, his admirable intellectual qualities, and, yes, even his limitations, accurately, and in considerable detail.

Obert's favorite title is professor. In spite of the need to work hard in his youth to help feed a large family, he skipped several grades in elementary and high school and entered the University of Utah at age sixteen. He has been on the fast intellectual track ever since!

Obert was uniquely qualified to teach philosophy and religion to university students. Prior to his university career he had served his church as a missionary, a teacher, and an author. His book, *Christ's Ideals for Living,* is now in its eighth printing. Its approach is scholarly and its appeal universal. He has also written several other books on religion and character education, and numerous articles on a variety of subjects. His teaching, writing, and researching have prepared him well to identify religious claims and procedures he finds in conflict with the teachings and ideals of Christ.

As a child, Obert resolved never to be impoverished as an adult, a resolve that was strengthened during his college years. He wanted financial resources, not only to gain freedom from physical dependency on others, but also so that he could be sure of intellectual independence.

From a humble beginning he has built the largest and most successful manufacturer of emblematic jewelry in the country, if not the world. For Obert it has always seemed natural to share his business success with others. His high regard for his employees is reflected in the numerous benefits he has provided, in the beautifully decorated corporate headquarters building, and the stunning retail store in Salt Lake City.

Obert has also served with distinction a number of civil and governmental agencies. He was chairman of the Utah American Revolution Bicentennial Commission when the Symphony Hall and the Salt Lake Art Center were constructed and the Capitol Theatre restored. Obert contributed greatly both in time and resources to complete these beautiful facilities.

He was an early member and promoter of the United Nations both locally and nationally. He advocated exchanges between the United States and the Soviet Union in the interest of peaceful cooperative relations, and lectured throughout Utah in favor of the UN.

Self-reliant and independent, Obert is known for freely speaking out about his convictions, regardless of the consequences. He has spent a lifetime teaching people to be individuals and to be understanding of others. He loves the life of the mind and freedom of thought and expression. He questions conclusions based on authority and dogma. His striving to know is insatiable and has resulted in a lifetime of study and teaching.

When individuals or groups conspired to block the priorities he cherished, he vigorously opposed such efforts. For this reason, his writings encourage and inspire teachers and others who may have been unjustly treated or degraded. His recently published public addresses, *One Man's Search,* reveal a disciplined and independent mind, always in search of the nature of truth.

His marriage to Grace Adams was fortunate. He sees it as providential. Initially attracted to her beauty, vivacity, and personality, he soon came to appreciate her many other sterling qualities. Their early married years entailed one move after another while he studied at Stanford and Harvard. This must have been hard on a young mother with babies. Her husband was imaginative and restless. She has been a competent, loving mother and companion; modest, gracious, and unassuming, with great warmth of personality. They both prize and cultivate lasting friendships.

Obert's father, Joseph Marion Tanner, was brilliant. He had an illustrious academic career, cut short by his deep involvement with Mormon polygamy, even after the church had abandoned the practice. Obert's mother, Annie Clark Tanner, daughter of a prominent polygamist family, was also a gifted and resourceful individual. Her autobiography tells of the intense personal indignities she suffered and the sacrifices she made because of her devotion to principle.

Obert asserts that a loving and intimate relationship between a mother and her children is the key to nurturing responsible adults. His strong conviction on this matter reflects his own intimate association with a loving mother. He has the same adoration for Grace and their children. Together they have known grief, sorrow, and suffering of mind and body, as well as joy and fulfillment.

Obert's autobiography makes inspired reading. It is a direct, intimate, and heartwarming glimpse of a truly magnificent human being.

M. Lynn Bennion
September 1993

PREFACE

. . .

PREFACE

. . .

Writing an autobiography is not an easy undertaking. I have started and stopped many times. There are problems of memory, modesty, and selectivity, to name only a few. No wonder so few such books are written or published, and that still fewer have interest beyond immediate family members and descendants. But I decided finally to plunge in and enjoy the task, embracing my past, present, and even my hopes for the future.

All my life I have had a passion for freedom, and that is the primary and recurring theme of this narrative. One result of this passion is that I have enjoyed more than my share of adventure and variety. These two words are the first that come to mind when I think of what characterizes my journey.

About adventure, Harry Emerson Fosdick, the great American preacher, wrote:

> It is an amazing adventure to be born upon this wandering island in the sky and it is an adventure to leave it when death calls. To go to school, to make friends, to marry, to rear children, to face through life the swift changes of circumstance that no man can certainly predict an hour ahead, these are all adventures . . . every New Year we begin a

tour of exploration into a twelvemonth where no
man's foot has ever walked before. If we all love
tales of pioneers, it is because from the time we
are weaned to the time we die, life is pioneering.

I think it was my love for adventure that helped me
create the O. C. Tanner Company. I hoped the free enterprise
system would function better if management found meaningful ways to recognize the efforts of labor. When I began
to sell corporate awards three-score years ago, this was not a
familiar way of going about it. Still, entrepreneurs must be willing to take risks and live with uncertainties. I have loved the
adventure of it.

About variety, the English poet, Robert Browning, wrote
(in *Cleon*):

> *I have not chanted verse like Homer,*
> *Nor swept string like Terpander, no nor carved*
> *And painted men like Phidias and his friend:*
> *I am not great as they are, point by point.*
> *But I have entered into sympathy*
> *With these four, running these into one soul,*
> *Who, separate, ignored each others' art.*
> *Say, is it nothing that I knew them all?*

In my desire to "know them all," I found the study and
teaching of philosophy to be a discipline of great variety and
diversity. In it, I could search constantly for new possibilities, new ways of thinking. I also learned to explore, to live out
some of my values, and to encourage others to live out theirs.

But, as always, I return to the matter of freedom. About
the underlying value of freedom, a great leader of our time,
David O. McKay, wrote:

> Next to the bestowal of life itself, the right
> to direct that life is God's greatest gift to man . . .

Freedom of choice is more to be treasured than
any possession earth can give . . . Whether born in
abject poverty, or shackled at birth by inherited
riches, everyone has this most precious of all life's
endowments, the gift of free agency, man's inherited and inalienable right.

Why is freedom so important? I think it is because, from
beginning to end, life is problem-solving, and we are likely to
solve our problems better with freedom than without it. When
I pondered a title for this autobiography, I decided on *One
Man's Journey in Search of Freedom* because, on the one
hand, I intend no example for others to follow. Each life is a
separate world, a different universe, unlike any other. But on
the other hand, there seems to be no more important quest
than the search for real freedom in life. This may be a value we
do all share, albeit in different ways.

In my own life, I wanted the freedom to solve the problems that were mine to solve. I hoped I would make worthy
choices, but choices that would not leave me less free tomorrow. There are no guarantees of course. We try to be thoughtful, lining up our options, reflecting on the consequences; then
we make a decision, and hope for the best. Sometimes one freedom leads to another freedom. Sometimes we subordinate our
freedoms to a larger good. Sometimes, unaware, we give our
freedoms away.

Someone has said: "Liberty is always dangerous, but it
is the safest thing we have." It is safest because it gives us
chances to correct our mistakes and/or discover new, more
liberating possibilities. Freedom was there, encouraged and
protected at the beginning of my life. And now, at life's end,
I cherish it above all else. I wouldn't change a thing.

I want to express my gratitude to those who have helped
in the preparation of this book: Dionne Williams, my patient
and excellent secretary; Margery Ward and Jack Wixom, editors
of great sensitivity and experience; and Lowell Durham of

the Humanities Center at the University of Utah, a longtime friend and colleague, who brought both professional skill and extraordinary wisdom to this project.

I am also deeply grateful for the support and encouragement over many years offered by Don Ostler, CEO of the Tanner Company, and my trusted colleague and friend; my children, Joan, Carolyn, and David; and my life's companion, Grace, who for sixty-two years has kept everything in good balance.

Obert C. Tanner
September 1993

Chapter One

ROOTS

. . .

Chapter One

Roots

A ship in harbor is safe,

but that is not what ships are built for.

—John A. Shedd

. . .

Farmington

I was born in Farmington, Utah, September 20, 1904, the youngest of ten children. Fortunately for me, large families were considered a blessing at that time.

My early memories are of walking about a mile to the elementary school, located on the eastern foothills of Farmington. On the way to school, I passed the Davis County courthouse; the county jail, with its bars in the windows; the "big store" that sold most everything; the drugstore that sold ice cream cones; Mr. Rampton's blacksmith shop; the ticket office of the Bamberger Electric Railroad; and the small post office where mother frequently sent me for the mail. Her older children had gone to Canada to work on father's ranch, or elsewhere to find jobs. I recall that letters came infrequently, but that they were very important to my mother.

As its name implies, Farmington was a farming community. There were no child labor laws. On a farm, the only question was whether a child was big enough to do the job. I remember occasions when an inquiring farmer, looking for help, would ask me to stand up while he estimated my size and strength. In my early youth, I sometimes helped drive a team of horses pulling a load of hay from Farmington to Salt Lake City, twenty miles to the south. We would leave shortly after midnight, arrive at dawn, and unload the hay, which was destined to be stuffed in the leather collars of harnesses. The trip took about five hours each way, perhaps a little less on the return. I learned that horses pick up their pace on their way back to the barn and I was glad of it.

Geographically, Farmington is located between the majestic Wasatch Mountains on the east, and the Great Salt Lake on the west. I remember the beautiful sunsets created by dust storms on the great desert beyond the lake. Thirty thousand years before, Lake Bonneville, an ice-age ancestor of the Great Salt Lake, had begun to lay down the rich soil bed which sustained the crops of Mormon immigrants who came in 1847. Like most communities in the American West, Farmington owed its existence to a stream of water that flowed from the mountains. Homes in Farmington were located in a central cluster. From my upstairs bedroom window, on the east side of our house, I could look up to the high Wasatch range. The stream that made Farmington beautiful and productive was called Big Creek.

Like most children, I dreamed about the future, what it might hold for me. Sometimes I thought of my favorite tale, Nathaniel Hawthorne's, "Ernest and the Great Stone Face." In it Hawthorne describes a community awaiting the day when a good man, resembling the Great Stone Face on the mountain above the town, would come to lead them. Several visitors are at first thought to be this man, but are finally rejected. The people ultimately notice that Ernest, their native son, "is the likeness of the Great Stone Face." Hawthorne was saying that a dream or vision, held long enough, may cause the one who holds it to become like the ideal itself. I loved that story.

Farmington was a homogenous culture. Nearly all its inhabitants were members of the Church of Jesus Christ of Latter-day Saints (commonly called the Mormon or LDS church), and most attended services every Sunday. All community activities, for both young and old, were sponsored by the church. That religion provided the principal way of perceiving and of interpreting the world, its history and destiny. The community was close-knit, in the tradition of a New England Puritan village. Sin was mostly about sex or disobedience to religious authority. Once, a girl had a baby out of wedlock. It seemed to cast a cloud over the whole community.

The center of learning was the elementary school. And, under religious supervision, weekly classes were taught in the Young Men's and Young Ladies' Mutual Improvement associations. Occasionally a speaker would visit from Salt Lake City. I recall the visit of an "elocution" teacher who was suspect because of her religious liberalism. In 1921, I was graduated from nearby Davis County High School, where some of the faculty were noted for ideas that did not conform to the local belief system. Later, at the University of Utah, in classes of science, philosophy, history, literature, and psychology, my perspectives broadened with many intellectual surprises. In the Farmington of my youth, however, there were few if any social disturbances that might have generated serious questions, activism, or the thought of radical change. Many people kept silent on controversial subjects, trying to achieve harmony by avoiding arguments. But I was curious and wanted to learn all I could about the world and its people, so I listened with interest to various opinions.

Unconventional and nonconforming views did stir some controversy. One of them was polygamy, which had been officially abandoned by the Mormon church in 1890. When I was a child, of course, many polygamous marriages persisted. Most of these predated the Manifesto, a church order which banned the practice. A few Mormons, however, including some of my relatives, still entered into the forbidden covenant—known to the faithful as "the principle of plural or celestial marriage"— even well into the twentieth century.

My Father

My father, Joseph Marion Tanner, was born in Payson, Utah, in 1859. Later his family moved to Provo where he attended Brigham Young Academy, which became present-day Brigham Young University (BYU). Father was a teacher there when he met and courted my mother, one of his students. They were married in 1883. My mother, who came from a polygamous family and revered her own father, devoutly believed in plural marriage and freely chose to be the second wife of J. M. Tanner.

In the first part of his life, my father was eminently successful. He was a student prodigy, a very young college teacher, fluent in several languages, a college president, and commissioner of education for the LDS church. Upon his retirement as president of Brigham Young Academy in Logan, the faculty gave father a 14-karat gold watch. It was eventually given to me, and I prize it very much. When he retired as president of Utah State Agricultural College (now Utah State University), he was given a gold-headed cane with his name engraved on it.

Father attended Harvard along with several other brilliant young men, for whom he had been able to secure scholarships. They became professional leaders in Utah: John A. Widtsoe was president of Utah State Agricultural College, later president of the University of Utah, and an apostle in the Mormon church; George Thomas also served as president of the University of Utah; Clarence Snow, founder of the Salt Lake Clinic, was chairman of the board of regents of the University of Utah; Joseph Jensen became Utah state engineer and superintendent of public schools for Utah. My mother went to Cambridge and boarded some of them while they were in school.

Then in 1907, J. M. Tanner fled the country to avoid prosecution as a polygamist. He had taken a fourth and fifth wife after the Manifesto. As I reflect on my father's life, I can imagine the contrast it must have been for him to leave a respected position in Utah and become a farmer in the rolling hill country of southern Alberta. We may never fully understand why people practiced polygamy, especially the interplay of motives involved. Some probably did marry out of religious conviction, and some because of personal attraction. My guess is that with father, the motivation was on the side of attraction. Polygamy was encouraged when he first embraced it, especially among the elite in Utah, and I think my father allowed its social rewards to dignify his own desires.

The LDS church authorities esteemed my father highly. Mother told me that, in 1900, my father was sustained in the General Conference of the church, to seven different positions. One of them was first counselor to Joseph F. Smith in the general superintendency of the LDS Sunday Schools. Later, he must have known that a man of his prominence could not cling to polygamy without consequence, yet he made that choice. Still, the church never disfellowshipped or excommunicated J. M. Tanner, even despite his additional plural marriages. Father was close to many powerful men in the church, some of whom also did not give up easily either the belief in or the practice of polygamy. Father died in Lethbridge, Alberta, in 1927.

Granted a child's bias, I think I never met a man more distinguished in appearance than my father. He was about six foot two or three inches tall, well proportioned, with large brown eyes, a high forehead, an engaging smile, and a contagious laugh. Mother must have been greatly attracted to him. She was very bright. BYU president Karl G. Maeser called her the most brilliant of her class. I remember, however, her comment that while she didn't mind being one of three wives, she was disappointed when father took the fourth and fifth. Her story is well told in her own autobiography, *A Mormon Mother.*

Polygamy became a great problem, not only for the church, but indeed for the United States, for Congress, and for the Supreme Court. In the days of the practice of polygamy, national political success depended on the position candidates took on the "twin evils" as they were called, slavery and polygamy. Slavery cost us a war and decades as a divided nation. Polygamy was about as costly within the Mormon culture. Today, there is a determined splinter group of Mormons—perhaps as many as thirty thousand—who continue to practice polygamy.

In this century, prosecutors are unwilling to send polygamists to prison, as they did in the days of my grandfather. Ezra T. Clark, my mother's father, spent a year in the state penitentiary because of polygamy. The government simply gave him (and others like him) the choice of disowning his second wife's children or going to prison. He chose prison.

The Supreme Court today might not rule as it did in 1879 in the polygamy case of *Reynolds vs. United States.* In the Reynolds decision, the Court reasoned that while there is complete freedom in religion to *believe* whatever one wants to believe, there is not freedom to *practice* whatever one wants to practice. The Court used an analogy from the culture of India, where widows were burned on the death of their husbands. Such a practice would be unacceptable in the United States. Similarly, the Court held that religious freedom to believe in polygamy did not include the freedom to practice it. This was one of my first lessons on freedom and it touched my life deeply.

As I grew up and thought about it, I came to feel an aversion to polygamy. I was not bitter, not even vocal, but I felt strongly that monogamy was good and polygamy was not good. Of course, the whole institution of marriage and family is now variously considered and practiced, but my views on these matters remain quite conventional.

The following story, told about me by two of my cousins, may reveal something about my life as the child of a polygamous marriage. My father came to Farmington on the Bamberger Electric train, which stopped just a block from our home. On one occasion when I was about four years old, I followed him as he walked down the street from the station, happy for the chance to speak to him. Apparently he ignored me. My cousins said that all the way to the house I shadowed him, repeating: "This is Obert, father, don't you know me? This is Obert." It may be that his mind was absorbed with some difficult public problem or that he did not hear me.

Father did not come to our home very often in my memory, though he was in Utah frequently. Even after he went to Canada, he maintained a law office in the Templeton Building in Salt Lake. His few visits were special occasions, as, for example, when mother prepared a Thanksgiving dinner. He was always treated as a distinguished guest.

In 1980, I helped to publish *A Life Divided: The Biography of Joseph Marion Tanner, 1859–1927* by Margery W. Ward. One of my motives was to give my father credit for his eminent achievements in the field of education. As I reflected on the whole of his life, I concluded that even with his domestic problems and failures, he made a good try. He helped many young people with their education. He does not show up too well in the last part of his life and I did not know him in the first, but I am sure I would have been very proud of his professional accomplishment in those years.

My Mother

My mother had beautiful brown hair, even features, lovely searching eyes, an ever-present smile, a sense of humor, and an analytical mind. She was soft-spoken, modest, quietly gentle even in the most disturbing situations, and, of necessity, a tireless worker. But more telling than outward appearance was the inward beauty of a noble character, unmatched in my life by any other. All through her life she sustained a thoughtful dignity, in spite of her many tragic disappointments. While I consider that my father had some failures as a human being, my mother seemed to have none. I have always loved and esteemed her with all my heart and, like another American of an earlier generation, I can say, "All I am and hope to be, I owe to my angel mother."

I am not alone in my praise of Annie Clark Tanner. Mother wrote her autobiography in the last year of her life. Dale L. Morgan, a distinguished historian, considered this book to be "one of the monuments of Mormon literature," and in the decades since, his estimate has been confirmed.

Mother was alone when I was born. She told me she sent a messenger uptown to Annie Palmer, the postmistress, who was also a midwife, telling her to hurry down and help with my delivery. In 1904, father was at the pinnacle of his public career and so was probably in Salt Lake or elsewhere.

I imagine the neighbors had mixed feelings about another baby at the Tanner home. Already there had been nine children, and seldom a father at home to help. I may have been considered by some as a new burden to Annie Clark Tanner. Yet I doubt if any child was ever more fortunate than I, to be born to a woman so willing, so pleased, so proud, so able, so marked with the gifts of human greatness. I find it difficult to put into words the awe, reverence, and wonder, I feel for my mother, that in her modest circumstances, she was willing to have yet another baby, when she had already had nine. All my life I wanted her to be glad and pleased about me. I wanted to return joy to her for the existence she so willingly gave to me.

Mother seemed to love me as much as if I were her only child. Her children were her life. As the youngest, I was quite vulnerable but she never allowed an older brother or sister to punish me. When they were angry with me, they would sometimes say, "Give him a licking, mother. If you don't I will." And when they were about to try, I can still hear her say quietly with words of finality, "Don't you dare touch that boy!" and they never did.

Although all of us, from childhood, worked for our food and clothing, there was never much thought that we were less fortunate than any other family in the community, at least I never thought so. We never felt poor, partly because of our lovely home. In 1900, Ezra T. Clark had given his daughter

Annie an acre of land and sufficient funds to build a truly beautiful home. The two-story house had large windows and an elegant fireplace. Such a lovely home instilled pride and generated dignity in all of us, despite our comparative poverty.

Nearly all the neighbors were relatives of my mother, her brothers and sisters. While they provided no direct financial support, they gave us chances to work on their farms. I liked and respected all my relatives on Clark Street, some more than others. I do recall the embarrassment I felt, when our neighbor-cousins would gleefully chant:

James Town, Clark Street,
Tanner's Hotel, and Nothing to Eat.

They did not recite this jingle very often, though for years I did hear it occasionally. I do not recall fighting with my cousins about it. I simply cringed and turned away. A child can be easily hurt while still keeping his pride.

Mother combined personal dignity with a deep modesty. No queen could have been more self-possessed, no scholar more searching, and no saint more gentle and humble. While our poverty was sharp, it did not cut. And if humiliation was near, it never found a place within. We were not afraid of others, and were never sorry for ourselves.

Mother was proud of each of her children and also proud to have a family by such an illustrious husband. I think she may have been influenced in this by a consideration of eugenics. It is perhaps understandable that sometimes farm people, especially in that era, regarded eugenics as an important factor in the practice of polygamy, even a justification of it. Nevertheless, ours was virtually a single-parent family.

On his departure for Canada, my father told my mother that she would have to look to her "stalwart sons" for her support. The two oldest stalwarts ran away from home in their early teens. They got jobs on the railroad that took them to faraway places. I recall their brief visits home and my mother's joy at seeing them again. Some of us were too young to support ourselves, so mother did housework for neighbors. She also worked as a practical nurse.

At that time, babies were born at home and doctors required the new mother to remain in bed for two weeks. So, for several years, my mother was able to support her own family by leaving us, not only to take care of the mother and newborn infant, but also to do housework and cooking for the family she attended. It was hard physical work, and must have been a difficult vocation for a woman, separating her from her own children for two weeks at a time. She kept her suitcase packed. I vividly recall waking in the morning to find her gone and crying to my older sister, "If only she would tell us when she is going to leave." I was four or five years old, too young to know that babies are sometimes born in the middle of the night. Mother had to respond quickly to a doctor's call. When she left, I suppose she didn't want to wake us up.

A child accepts conditions as they are and I did not mind, at first, having no father at home. As I grew up and became aware of a normal family life in the homes of our neighbors, I came to feel misgivings about polygamy because of the way my father left my mother to fend for herself and her large family. I also came to feel a personal sense of loss.

Freedom in Our Family

I sensed that I was born into a world of great freedom. In early twentieth-century America, the limitations were few and the opportunities many. From an early age, I enjoyed this spirit of freedom at home. Mother held firmly to her philosophy that a child should have the largest possible measure of freedom. I do not remember that she ever asked for obedience. She didn't tell us to do something, but rather asked if we would like to do it. She gave liberally of her encouragement, and listened intently to each child's account of some personal achievement. One of my brothers commented on mother's patience and dignity: "She raised her family without raising her voice."

I think I developed most of my love of freedom from my mother. She won her own intellectual and spiritual freedoms gradually, but in her later life she became remarkably independent of institutional and domestic authority. We shared a love of books, lectures, and new ideas. She wanted to pass on a sense of independence to her children, possibly to spare us some of the pain of having to achieve our own intellectual emancipation. I recall she opposed my father's strong preference for domestic discipline. I remember her saying that a child was not really free, if not free to make a mistake. Her tolerance of my choices, and the lessons she taught by discussion and example, were constant influences. I do not recall, as I became mature, that she ever attempted to divert me from the decisions I made. As we sometimes discussed alternatives, I was aware that the final decision was my own.

Another priority so constant in mother's life, was the importance of education. A good education for her children was the single greatest goal of her life. Her autobiography makes this amply clear. I was caught up in this ambition and it became my own life's purpose as well. I spent half a century as a student and teacher in universities. In our home, around the dinner table, the freest of discussions took place. My brothers were nonconformists and this accounted for much of our discussion. We were scrutinized by many pillars of our community. While mother may have worried about us, she never counseled silence or conformity. She gave all she could for our education, apparently willing to accept whatever the results might be.

Members of Our Family

Each of my five older brothers thought highly of his own ideas. I listened with rapt attention as they related their daily experiences, especially their personal responses as to whether something seemed fair or foul, and what they intended to do about it. There was no father to control, advise, encourage, or admonish. I listened and learned from the freely expressed opinions and judgments of my older brothers, from their arguments, achievements, and failures.

Mother also had four daughters, including Belva, who died in early infancy from whooping cough, and Leah, who died at the age of three. Mother's oldest child, Jennie, had five children of her own before she died of a heart illness at the age of thirty-five. Lois, a twin sister to Leah, died at age seventy-one. She and I were close friends.

In the order of their ages, my memory of a special characteristic of each would be the following: Jennie's gentleness; Myron's friendliness; Herschel's keen observation of people; LaVinz's dissent; Kneland's critical bent; Sheldon's perfectionism; and Lois, for her likeness to mother. All were strong individuals and each quite different. I had good relations with all of them. For the last nineteen years, I have been the sole survivor of mother's ten children.

As I grew up, my mother and I became good friends in the best sense of the word. Our relationship was formal, something like that in traditional English families, where sentiment is quite restrained. I kissed my mother only upon taking a long leave, or returning from an extended absence. Her influence upon my life was as pervasive as the atmosphere itself. She enjoyed my two vocations of teaching and business, but mostly my teaching, being herself a good student and teacher.

Ancestors

The Tanners immigrated to this country six generations ago. My fourth great-grandfather, William Tanner, came from England in the 1670s, and settled in Rhode Island. My father's mother, Mary Jane Mount, was a descendent of Jean Guilliaume Bessác, who came from France with Lafayette during the Revolutionary War. He did not return to France after the war; but settled in Hudson, New York. John Tanner (b. 1778), my great-grandfather, is the best known of our Tanner ancestors. He was a successful farmer. His large and imposing home, of southern style architecture, still stands on the shores of beautiful Lake George in New York.

John Tanner was converted to Mormonism in 1831. He sold all his property and moved his large family to Kirtland, Ohio, turning over a considerable sum in gold coins to Joseph Smith, the leader of his newly found religion. John Tanner then migrated with the Saints from Kirtland to Missouri, then to Illinois, then to Nebraska, and finally to Salt Lake City, where he died in 1850.

Myron Tanner, my grandfather, was a member of the Mormon Battalion in the war with Mexico. He became ill and was sent to Pueblo, Colorado, where he was discharged. He then traveled to the Great Salt Lake Valley, arriving four days after Brigham Young. He later settled in San Bernardino, California, and did well in mining and livestock. Returning to Utah in 1855, he met and proposed marriage to Mary Jane Mount. After they were married, they settled in Payson, Utah. Then the family moved to Provo where my grandfather prospered with a flour mill and was part owner of the Provo Woolen Mills. He was bishop of the Third Ward in Provo and a member of the first board of education of Brigham Young Academy, later BYU.

On my mother's side, my fifth great-grandfather, George Clark, also came from England. He settled in Connecticut in the 1630s. My great-great-grandfather, John Clark II, was a soldier in the Revolutionary War. His son (my great-grandfather), Timothy Baldwin Clark, was a soldier in the War of 1812. He built the first frame residence in what later became the city of Chicago. Clark Street in that city is named after him. His son was my grandfather, Ezra Thompson Clark (1823–1901). The descendants of Ezra T. Clark now live in many parts of the country. Some of them, including Merlin Olsen, of football and television fame, have become quite distinguished.

Ezra T. Clark was an unusually successful businessman. But far more remarkable was his success as a polygamist. Two of his wives lived across the street from each other. My mother was the oldest child in the second family. Near the end of his life, Ezra T. Clark met with his wives and twenty children. In a large hat, he placed descriptions of his properties, deeds, and securities. He held his hat so his children could not see, and each child drew two pieces of paper—one describing land and the other securities. This was the way he divided his rather large estate.

My mother wrote *A Biography of Ezra Thompson Clark,* published in 1931. It is a Utah pioneer story about a man of profound love and loyalty for his family and his church. At the conclusion of the distribution of his property he gave this counsel: "To my wives and children: . . . I would not have my family suppose that I esteem money as I esteem honor. . ."

Perhaps the most important thing to be said about my Mormon roots, my birth heritage, is that I was cherished as a child and I learned to cherish my family in turn. Polygamy seems such a troublesome practice to us, one might expect nothing but ill to come of it. Perhaps more in spite of it than because of it, however, the Mormon religion places great importance on the family and I was very much a beneficiary of that teaching and practice. I mention it here because in our present culture where "family values" are much debated, the goodness of ordinary love, responsibility, and loyalty, is not to be taken for granted.

Chapter Two

EARLY YEARS

. . .

Chapter Two

Early Years

This above all . . . to thine own self be true.

—William Shakespeare

▪ ▪ ▪

Uncle Eddy's Farm

I worked on my Uncle Eddy's farm from the time I was six until I was twelve. Edward Clark was a very successful farmer. He had, among other things, one of the largest dairy farms in Davis County. He was a hard worker and, in my opinion, his three sons, Eddy, Rulon, and Orson, worked even harder. Uncle Eddy and his wife, Aunt Wealthy, were people of fine character, very frugal and profoundly religious. I mention frugality because they always served water to drink at the table, although their dairy farm shipped fifty to sixty gallons of milk every morning to Salt Lake. It was a peaceful family— no quarreling, no unkind remarks. I can't recall a time when I was scolded by them, though once in a while my cousins teased me, which I never liked. But I was fond of them, and I know they liked me.

The approval of my cousins was important to me. I tried hard to please them and I know I was an asset to their farm. I was never told to *go* to the toolroom in the barn and get something; I was always told to *run* and get it. Always it was run, and I ran. Some years later, someone overheard my cousin, Rulon Clark, the respected juvenile-court judge, say of me, "Obert was the hardest worker I ever knew." Those days, now long past, are still vivid in my memory.

Our nearby home was a place to sleep and eat and study. Sometimes in the summer, when my mother was away in Salt Lake on a nursing case, I lived for brief periods with Uncle Eddy's family. In the morning I would drive the cows to pasture, some two or three miles away, and then, in the evening, drive them home for milking. Sometimes a bull would be with the herd and I had to keep my distance. Occasionally a second bull would join, and this usually meant a fight. Their battles were noisy and sometimes bloody, so I was relieved whenever I was given a horse to ride.

Grass grew profusely along the railroad right-of-way, and so my uncle took advantage of this grazing area. He had me herd the cows all day along the railroad tracks. A major part of my job was to ensure there were no cows on the track when high-speed transcontinental passenger trains went screaming by. Sometimes, sitting all day on my horse on a hot summer day, I would get sleepy and my vigilance would lapse. The engineer on the train would then shake his finger or fist at me as he looked down from his high cab, sometimes applying his screeching brakes and blowing his whistle non-stop. My uncle or cousins would thus become aware of pending disaster, and have clear proof of my negligence.

One morning the "Yellowstone Special" came within a few seconds of hitting a line-up of my uncle's best milk cows. They were on their way to get a drink at a nearby stream and ignored my frantic efforts to get them off the tracks. I was crying when my uncle rode up on his horse, and in a soft voice said, "Well, my boy, that's one way to learn!" I was grateful he didn't scold me. I must have learned, because that particular scene was never repeated. None of the cows in my care was ever lost to a train, although occasionally we did find other smelly carcasses of such unfortunates, and covered them with earth.

I was six years of age—too young to mount a horse by myself—when I was first given the tiring and unpleasant task of riding and guiding the horse that pulled the hayfork. This fork would lift a load from a hayrack wagon so that it could be dumped on a large stack for the animals' winter consumption. As I turned the horse around, my slightest inattention would bring forth a loud shout from the one loading the hayfork, or the one dumping the hay on the stack. A small error could have buried either one of them in hay.

Riding back and forth all day in the hot sun, I was miserable. I remember that the men found me a large straw hat. They made so much fuss about what a fine hat it was that I was persuaded to stay with the job. The hayfork workhorse was a huge animal compared to the horse I rode to drive the cows. His back was so broad it seemed almost flat to me. I well remember when I gathered enough courage to jump off that horse—a fair distance, or so it seemed to me. Some days, thirty loads were added to one of the large stacks of hay. My cousins counted and were proud of the number.

As I grew older, I was promoted from driving and herding cows, to cleaning out their stalls and filling their mangers with hay. I also fed pigs the skim milk from the separator, but my most important job was helping to milk the herd. Milking at that time was done by hand. There were no machines. At the age of seven, I was given "Old Three-Tit" to milk. She was a tame Guernsey cow, with one teat much larger than the others. I worked on this largest teat with both of my child's hands. Her milk flowed despite my lack of strength. Eventually another cow was added to my responsibilities, and another, and another. At first, my cousins would follow me to "strip" the cows—getting the last and best of the milk with their stronger hands.

To break the monotony of this twice-daily job, I would sometimes engage one of my cousins, who was milking nearby, in conversation. One day one of them told me, "Don't talk so much, Obert." I was hurt and quite subdued by his blunt criticism. Many years later this same cousin left the farm to teach in a junior high school. He registered in a class I was teaching at the university. I couldn't help reflecting that now, as my student, he could no longer tell me to stop talking.

I may have been too proud of my milking ability. On one occasion, my cousins talked me into milking a young heifer called "Toothpick the Third." She was mean and it was necessary to chain her legs while she was being milked. My cousins thought she might be tame enough without chains, and they agreed I was to be the one to find out. She wasn't. She kicked me in the eye so hard I fell into the gutter, spilled the milk, and was covered with manure. I was wild with rage, or so I remember. I thought my cousins had deliberately set me up. "You knew she would kick!" I yelled at them. At first they laughed, quite heartily as I remember. But then my tears and appearance sobered them. I was too proud to walk off the job. I stayed and finished milking my share of the herd, ignoring their solicitations. I had a black eye for days.

At times the work may have been too hard for me. I remember my mother snatching me away and sending me to my Aunt Sarah's home in Salt Lake when my Aunt Mariah complained: "They're killing Obert, Annie. They're working him to death." But after a week of rest and playing in Liberty Park, I was back on the job with my three cousins. I felt that my honor was at stake. I didn't want to be a quitter. I think I was then about nine years old.

Working on my Uncle Eddy's dairy farm gave me the experience of helping to support the family. After one of my first jobs, picking up potatoes, my uncle looked down at me and asked:

"How much do I owe you, my boy?"

"Whatever you say, uncle," was my reply.

"Well, would a nickel be all right?"

"Yes sir," I answered. I was genuinely delighted.

Every day after school I was expected to spend several hours cleaning stables and feeding the animals. For this I was given a pail of milk. There would be no evening meal at home until I arrived with my load. On one occasion, one of my cousins gave me such a small measure from the large bucket that I burst into tears as soon as I was out of sight of the milk house. I cried all the way home and when my mother asked what on earth was the trouble, I pointed to my small portion.

She said, "Did he ask if that were all right?"

"Yes," I replied.

"What did you answer?"

"I said it was all right."

My mother must have been more distraught with my tears than with the poor pay. Searching for some wisdom that might protect me from another heartbreak, she quoted Shakespeare's famous lines from *Hamlet*. "Now you must remember," she said, "To thine ownself be true, and it must follow as the night the day, thou canst not then be false to any man."

Even though I understood that I had not been true to myself in telling my cousin I was satisfied, I never could bring myself to complain or protest whatever I was given. Nevertheless, I may have learned something intended by Shakespeare: It is not an easy admonition to live by.

Later, besides earning milk, I took my pay in produce: a sack of potatoes for working in the potato field, or a box of peaches for picking peaches, and, rarely, a piece of meat cut from a slaughtered animal.

At the time of my first paid work, my two oldest brothers had left home, probably to escape the confusion and labor in a large family. When they returned for brief visits they made a great fuss over me for the food and coal I helped bring home. I remember how they raised their voices in lavish praise. My oldest brother, Myron, had a way of speaking in superlatives, and I can almost hear him now, raising his voice in amazement to credit me with my bucket of milk. "Look at that kid, mother. Look at what he has done. He's earned all that milk. What do you know about that? Look at that kid!" "Earning milk" became a cheerful routine for me. I blossomed under such praise. It was heady stuff for a small boy to have so many compliments heaped upon him. I realize now my older brothers, home for a fleeting visit, wanted to see us get by as best we could.

One of my first memories is of my mother tucking me into bed with a blanket I had helped to earn. My mother and sister and probably a brother or two were present when I was wrapped in that luxury. I cannot recall how I earned the money to purchase it, but the memory of my first enjoyment of it is almost as vivid today as it was so many years ago.

Picking up Coal

In the age of coal-burning railroad steam engines, we searched for discarded coal along the railroad tracks. When I was too small to lift some of the larger pieces, my job was to find them in the snow along the tracks, and mark them in some way so that my older brothers could locate them. They would put the pieces of coal in sacks, and pull the sacks home on a sled. As a child, I became expert in distinguishing coal from the black rock-slate that appeared to be coal but was much heavier and less combustible. The firemen on the loco- motives threw off the slate. My job was to find the pieces of real coal that occasionally rolled off the top of the tenders as the firemen shoveled it into the firebox of the engine.

For several years, we obtained fuel for our home furnace this way, scouring a stretch of the tracks about five miles long, between Kaysville and Centerville. I came to know these tracks quite well. I still remember that the best place to find coal was on a curve of the tracks, or next to the water tank. When I was older, I became self-conscious about this enter- prise. I tried not to be seen by my cousins, who crossed the tracks with loads of hay for the livestock in the fields below. When they did see me, they would sometimes call out some remark that embarrassed me. I recall hiding back of the water tank when they drove by.

Once my mother told me I was wanted by the manager of our local store. I went up the street to the store, about a half mile away. The manager took me upstairs to his office and from a window pointed out the building across the street that was the county jail. He asked me how I would like to be locked up there. I was terrified. I remember so well the bars on the doors and windows of that building. Not until I returned home did I learn that the store owner thought I had stolen his coal from a railroad car located on one of the side tracks.

My mother tells the story as she recalled it in her autobiography:

> The little boys picked up coal off the railroad tracks at the place where it was unloaded from the cars into wagons. Obert, who was eight years old that winter, saw some coal on the ground at the Commercial Store where much of it was stored and sold to customers. So he took his little express wagon up there for coal. But the coal was on store property. He was asked to come inside, where from the window, the county jail was in full view.
>
> "That is where boys go who steal," said the store manager to the surprised boy.
>
> I give this illustration to show how adults misunderstand the motives of a child. I did not know the little fellow had gone up there. I was so humiliated about our condition that I made no explanation.

Her last sentence here tells a great deal about the attitude with which we met our situation. Being silent was mother's way of facing poverty.

Lessons of Poverty

Countless families live in poverty and they learn to adjust quite well. As a child, I did not realize that life for my mother was a desperate struggle. She was too proud to ask her brothers for help, and too protective to let her children know their actual situation. When I was very young, and mother wasn't home, I would make the rounds of the neighbors' homes to find her, sometimes discovering her scrubbing their floors to buy us food. This made a deep impression on me. I was not aware how little she was paid, but I did know it was necessary for her to earn money. Six of us were then living at home. Mother's autobiography reads, "I worked for the neighbors, washed, cleaned house, even painted. Part of my pay was in milk. Work was cheap in the country, so fifteen cents an hour was all that I received, no matter what the job."

Sometimes in those years there simply was not enough food for all of us. We never had meat, except an occasional fifteen cents' worth, and that only for my older brother, LaVinz, when he was doing very hard work. I was sometimes sent to the store with the fifteen cents to purchase meat for his lunch. If anyone in the family were sick, he might sometimes be favored with some ice cream. The drugstore man didn't like to put one scoop in a carton, all for a nickel, but an ice cream cone would be nearly melted before I could get home with it. I was quite embarrassed when I had to insist he put it in a carton. One store refused to give us credit, but the other store helped us when we were in desperate need. That store owner, J. D. Wood, himself a polygamist, would be just as generous as our risky finances allowed. Generally we would pay something on the long overdue account, and then the next day charge some more.

Our basic diet was bread and milk and bottled fruit. Breakfast was hot graham mush spread over pieces of bread with cream or milk, and lots of sugar. Another part of our diet was graham gems, or, on special occasions, some genuine English Yorkshire pudding cooked in a large square pan in the oven. My mother was an expert at making this treat, a talent she learned, no doubt, from her English mother.

When I did not have shoes to wear, my feet were wrapped in cloth. I told people at school that the floor had slivers that hurt. I remember two or three teachers examined my feet wrapped, but I didn't feel conscious of any neglect. Seeing my mother scrub the neighbors' floors, and the fact that she had to leave us for two weeks at a time to work as a nurse, made deep and lasting impressions on me. I suppose poverty gave me the great respect I had for any job I could rustle. I am sure it gave me the determination, later on, to make the O. C. Tanner Company as successful as possible.

Early School Days

I have warm feelings about my school days in Farmington. The elementary school was high on a hill near the mountains, about a fifteen-minute walk from our home. There were no school lunches. We took sandwiches in a paper bag, or sometimes ran the mile home during the noon hour.

When I was in the fourth grade, my mother moved her family to Salt Lake, thinking we might have some contact with father, who had a law office in town and made occasional visits from Canada. Mother hoped he would help with our support. She was mistaken. Father never paid us a visit in our modest home on K Street.

One unpleasant memory was an assignment to go to the Royal Baking Company on Third South and buy day-old bread for half price, a nickel for two loaves. I carried a package of six loaves tied together with a string. I recall the string hurt my fingers. It was more than a mile back to K Street. Once some boys made fun of me and scattered my loaves of bread on the sidewalk. I was nine years old.

At that time I attended Longfellow School, where the teacher insisted that I be put back a grade to a younger class. It was a traumatic experience. I held on to my desk when the teacher tried to pry me loose and send me to the room of a lower grade. As we marched in from recess every noon, I had to dodge my teacher's attempts to block me from entering her room. I couldn't bear the disgrace of being demoted. On the playground I was snubbed because of my low rating with the teacher. My peers wouldn't choose me to be on their side for a softball game. My sister, Jennie, and the principal had a meeting with my teacher. I recall I was able to answer their questions on geography. That saved me from a demotion. This miserable time in my life suddenly ended when the roof on our house in Farmington burned, and we had to move back to our more friendly hometown.

Paying a Dentist Bill

The dentist described my teeth as "just like chalk." By the time I was ten years of age I must have held a record for the largest number of fillings, including two gold crowns. I would go to Salt Lake each Saturday to Dr. Cook, who did all he could to save my teeth. The bill must have been very high.

One day he asked me when and how I could pay him. I replied that I didn't know, that I was working for my uncle. Then with a need to get something for all his work, he said, "If you will get ten dollars by tomorrow, that will be all I will charge." He was an old man, and I recall he would stop grinding, to my great relief, and lie down on a couch next to his dental chair. I liked him, and I wanted to pay him. So without consulting anyone, I went directly to my Uncle Eddy and made the proposition that I would work for him all summer if he would give me ten dollars to put in the mail to my dentist.

My uncle was hesitant about such an arrangement. He called in his three boys and they cross-examined me to see if

I really would keep my end of the bargain. Finally my uncle gave me a check for ten dollars. I will never forget my great satisfaction, as I handed the envelope containing that check to the clerk in the mail car of the passenger train that stopped in Farmington every morning. I had no problem keeping my part of the bargain. I was ten years old and thought working all summer was a fair exchange for ten dollars. It was my first experience with anything like a labor contract.

A Christmas Tree

That same year, or possibly the year before, my mother took my sister and me to Salt Lake to celebrate Christmas with my sister, Jennie. Jennie's husband taught piano lessons for a living. They had five children and lived in a very modest home at the upper end of Sixth Avenue. We arrived on Christmas Eve. They were simply too poor to afford a Christmas tree, but I remember we brought with us some modest presents. Mother was very fond of preparing for Christmas. Not having a tree bothered me. Then I remembered some small change I had. To save car fare, I walked from Jennie's home down to Third South and State Street. I didn't tell anyone I was going, but simply slipped away in search of a Christmas tree.

It was several miles to the downtown district where Christmas trees were sold on the street. It was rather late in the evening. In fact, when I arrived, the downtown stores were closing and the crowds dispersing to go home. I found someone selling trees, though only a few were left. I told the man I wanted to buy one and showed him all my change. At first he offered me a rather small tree. Then, changing his mind I suppose, since the time for selling Christmas trees was ending, he gave me a bargain of almost the biggest tree he had. That still left me with car fare. I thought the bigger the better, but I didn't think of the problem of getting it to my sister's home.

When a Sixth Avenue streetcar stopped, I tried to get on where the passengers entered at the rear, but the conductor taking fares simply refused to let me get on with my large Christmas tree. As I backed away, I must have looked very disconsolate. Someone said, "Why don't you get on at the front end?" A man carried my tree to the front of the streetcar and said to the motorman, "Let this kid on with his Christmas tree." The motorman refused, and suddenly something possessed the crowd, an awareness, I suppose, of a small child with a burden too heavy for him to carry, trying to move it the only way he could. It was Christmas Eve. I recall a number of passengers shouting at the motorman, "Let the kid on!" I was almost lifted with the tree, and pushed on the streetcar, despite the motorman's protests. People caught the spirit of Christmas and crowded together to make room for me and my tree. The tree was a Colorado Blue Spruce, similar to the kind we cut in Farmington Canyon. It had sharp needles. I was aware it made those around me in the streetcar very uncomfortable. I was mortified over the discomfort I was causing, but everyone seemed to put up with it in good spirit.

The snow was deep when I got off the streetcar. It was all I could do to drag the tree to my sister's home. When I came through the front door, my mother looked incredulous. "Where did you get that tree?" she asked. She was unable to understand how I came to possess it. While she always believed what I told her, or at least I think she did, I could tell she was quite perplexed. Of course, it was a happy Christmas for all of us. We made a stand for the tree and decorated it with ornaments cut from paper of various colors. I recall I felt I was not much less than a real hero.

Miss Harding, My Best Teacher

Despite my native curiosity and my generally positive feelings about school, I was not a good student in the early elementary years. I was in trouble with almost every teacher and with a good many of my classmates. Small children can sometimes be quite cruel. I remember well how I had to fight other boys after school, possibly because they were aware I had no father to stand up for me. Once I had seen a boy refuse to defend himself, and he took a severe beating. I resolved that this would never happen to me. In any case, I stood up for myself and determined never to start a fight but also never to back away from one. With such a policy, it is needless to add that I had several fights after school, usually by previous arrangement, which many of the students came to watch. It is an unhappy memory for it was a painful experience. I never cared for a show of violence.

I recall the teachers were silently supportive of me when I was fighting a boy with the reputation of being a bully. We fought every day after school for a week. Finally, somebody suggested that we call it even and shake hands. I was more than willing. I am not proud of such events in my life. They just happened and I accepted them.

My fifth-grade teacher gave up and insisted I go to another room. I was assigned to a teacher named Elizabeth Harding. She was an unmarried woman and quite plain in appearance. One might say her beauty was within. She was very serious, the essence of conscientiousness, and she ran a tight ship. There was no fooling around; there was work to be done and she got on with it in a very straightforward manner. Miss Harding taught both fifth and sixth grades in one room, as was then common in small schools. She must have had a pretty low opinion of me, considering the way in which I came to be in her class, and was determined that I would not give her a bad time. Sure enough, a bad time started, and she sent me to the principal's office for disciplining. (I believe she thought I'd get a good whipping.)

The principal, G. Q. Knowlton, took me to a small room filled with books and there he picked up a whip like the ones used by jockeys in horse races. He made this whip very visible as he walked up and down in front of me, lashing the leg of his trousers. I grew angrier by the moment and when it appeared he might hit me, I openly defied him. I told him with some feeling he didn't dare whip me! He stared at me and I thought I saw a smile on his face. "Why don't I dare whip you?" he asked. I replied, "just because you don't. Don't you dare touch me!" Then I could see he was smiling a little more and soon he sat down and we were having a friendly chat. We talked about my problem, which I now think was boredom, and about my bad conduct. I told him I would do better, and there was no whipping. This incident may reveal something of a deep inner pride I learned from my mother.

Back in the classroom, my teacher, Miss Harding, had classified me with two other problem boys, and I can still hear their names repeated along with mine. Frequently she would intone: "Obert, James, and Jeffy, pass out in the hall!" The three of us would get up and march out. We stood around outside the classroom for what seemed like a long time. The next day, it was the same thing, "Obert, James, and Jeffy, pass out in the hall!"

Perhaps one reason for my school difficulties was our home life. My mother would be away from home a great deal in her work as a practical nurse, and this left five of us to take care of ourselves. My sister, Lois, just older, did all the cooking and baking. Mother tells in her own story that Lois began baking bread when she was nine years old. On one occasion I recall my mother telling me that she had told my teacher she needed to have help from the school in raising her family. She said she would put her children at their disposal, and whatever the teacher decided should be done, she would support. She expressed her hope they would give her whatever help they could. I suppose one could say this was a rather desperate plea from a mother.

In any case, my teacher, Miss Harding, began to take an interest in me. She would keep me after school to talk to me.

At first she scolded me for what I had done that day. Then, she began telling me of some assets I had that she thought showed some hope. I remember one thing she said that really shocked me. She said, "Obert, Stuart Gardner (he was the pride of her class), will never be a great man as you may some day become, but he is a fine student, and he does well. You should try to do as well."

I remember the surprise I felt when she said this. I was sure I was the opposite of Stuart in every way. He was good; I was bad. He could write well; I couldn't. He won the spelling matches; I didn't. He could sing well in song practice; I refused to sing. No contrast could have been sharper—at least in my mind—and now the teacher was telling me that some day I might be a greater man. I simply couldn't believe what she had said. Then I began to wonder if perhaps I could do a lot better and maybe amount to something. That was a turning point in my young life and so began a lifetime friendship with Miss Harding.

Twenty years later, when I was a speaker at Granite School District's fall teacher convention, I told them about the best teacher I ever had, never dreaming Miss Harding was in the audience. She was then teaching at Granite Junior High School. I was glad she heard me express my gratitude to her publicly. Miss Harding died at age ninety-six, and at her request I spoke at her funeral. It was on my seventy-fifth birthday. I said, "Miss Harding loved me, and I loved her." Our friendship had lasted from the time she taught me in the fifth grade. Grace and I invited her to our home for dinner when she retired from teaching.

Another pleasant school experience in those early years in Farmington was when the principal, who also taught both the seventh and eighth grades, gave me a special promotion at mid-year from the seventh to the eighth grade. At the time I was very pleased. I was not aware that, with this promotion, I might be losing my social life with some of my best friends. More of such gain and loss followed when I skipped a year in high school. The principal of the high school once called me a "credit factory." I began studies at the University of Utah at sixteen. That, too, may have been a social mistake. It may be better to stay with one's peers.

In my years of high school, our home evenings were times of uninterrupted study. I recall one of our neighbors saying to my mother, "I declare, Annie, when I come over to see you, I walk around the house and it is as quiet as a library."

As a youth I had many dreams and hopes, and, I might add, an abundance of ambition. My older brother, Kneland, described the following incident at the family dinner table. He said he had asked my seventh-grade teacher, G. Q. Knowlton, if he ever noticed me silently looking out the window of the classroom. Mr. Knowlton said he had noticed this.

"Do you know what he is thinking about when he just gazes out the window?"

"No," replied my teacher, "what is he thinking about?"

"He's thinking about the future glory of Obert."

I was terribly embarrassed.

Bicycling through Utah

When I was eleven years old, my brother, LaVinz, home-steaded some land in southwestern Colorado. He had me join him in driving a team of horses and a wagon of supplies from Salt Lake City. While we were traveling, LaVinz was not very talkative and I became bored riding in the wagon so I took off and hiked over mountains and canyons to see all I could along the way. On one of my solo trips over some mountains, I rolled a large rock down a hill. It landed between the railroad tracks. I was in a state of panic until I was able to move it away.

On this long wagon trip, we had to earn our way. Things got tough for us financially. In Price we got a job jacking up a large storage bin of wheat. It was dangerous work but with hydraulic jacks we were able to do the job. We simply didn't have the money to feed both of us, so my departure was necessary. I used the money I had earned to buy a second-hand bicycle and rode it back to Salt Lake from Price, a distance of a hundred miles.

When my brother-in-law, Lynn R. Fairbanks, was traveling from house to house teaching piano, he noticed a large field planted with sugar beets. He asked the owner for a job for me. I didn't mind this job, though I had to work alone all day, thinning and hoeing in a large beet field. The farm was located in Taylorville, about five miles west of Ogden. When I went home on Sundays, I rode my bicycle to the Bamberger train in Ogden, and then returned to my job late on Sunday. It would be near midnight and it seemed that every house had a dog, and every one of them growled, barked, and sometimes snapped at me. These midnight bicycle rides were thoroughly miserable experiences.

Later, I had a better experience on a bicycle when I won the town's fourth of July race. I wore coveralls while the other riders stripped down. I heard the bishop say to my mother: "I am glad the boy with his clothes on won the race."

Herding Sheep in Canada

When I was thirteen and my sister, Lois, was fifteen, she and I were put on the train bound for father's ranch about seven miles southeast of Woolford, Alberta. My older brother, Kneland, who liked to manage other people's lives, made a deal with father, that if we were sent to Canada for the summer to help him on the ranch, father would pay a large store bill we had in Farmington, a debt which was probably long overdue.

I was bitterly disappointed about being taken out of the eighth grade before I was graduated, mostly because I would miss athletic contests in which we were participating against other eighth-grade classes throughout Davis County. I was proud to be on the baseball team. We had won almost every game and the final championship was coming up. Also, we were preparing for the annual track meet to be held in Kaysville. For me, that eighth-grade school year was a year of fun and glory. The principal liked me and I liked everybody. My timely arrival in Canada, however, apparently made some difference to my father, whose negotiations with my brother required me to leave school early in April.

In that year of 1918, World War I was reaching a climax. Farm help was scarce. When we arrived, Lois was given the job of cooking for about a dozen ranch workers. I was assigned to help care for a herd of about two thousand sheep. It was just past lambing time and I was immediately initiated in the work of docking and tailing the new lambs. I recall how much I would have preferred the work that was given to my half-brother, Walton, namely, plowing and harrowing land for grain. I liked to work with horses and had done similar work on Uncle Eddy's farm.

A severe drought afflicted Alberta in 1918. Livestock had to be shipped to the slaughter yards for lack of feed. Wheat fields turned brown and yellow when the grain was just a few inches high. To preserve livestock, the government agreed to ship farm animals, free of charge, to the mountains, where feed was available. Accordingly, our sheep were loaded on a long livestock train and we headed for Crow's Nest Pass. This was in the high mountains on the border between Alberta and British Columbia. We unloaded the sheep at Blairmore and began to trail them into the mountains where we had been allocated an area suitable for grazing, some thirty-five miles from the railroad.

My job was to cook all the meals for Tom Muckle, the sheepherder, and myself. I was also to move camp, and make the trip on my horse for camp supplies. Each trip I made was a fairly long journey. The sheepherder and I trailed the sheep through thick forests to the open spaces created by lightning fires. In these open spaces, peavine flourished, good feed for the sheep. My cooking, over an open fire, consisted mostly of flapjacks. We covered them with jam, and had tea to drink. At night the coyotes and wolves howled. We were in wild country. I felt some fear, but I carried a thirty-two revolver. At that time, I think no other herd of sheep had penetrated so far north from the railroad at Crow's Nest Pass.

I was assigned to do a man's work, but I was ill prepared. I was terrified of wild animals, and lonely to the point of despair. Frequently I would cry, sometimes several times a day. At one point, just after we had unloaded the sheep, I began to weep. I had been surprised when told by Tom Muckle what I was expected to do. There were no paths or trails to follow. Through my tears, I saw father standing in some bushes, a short distance away. I wiped my eyes and took a few steps towards him to see if he were really there. I was not mistaken. He stared at me, but said nothing, offered no comfort or reprieve, and left the next day. Seeing my father watch me cry, knowing that he knew of my unhappiness yet offered nothing that a father might say or do for a child, was traumatic for me. I could not feel any affection for him.

We stopped to eat at a logging camp before father left us. The cook was a middle-aged lady who sized up our situation and scolded my father with real anger when she learned that I was to be left in that country at my tender age. Father just laughed at her scolding. He explained that he wanted to make a man out of me. She was not persuaded. Looking back, I believe that my father needed me as a economic asset and "making a man out of me" was more an excuse. Nevertheless, one day, months later, I started to cry and no tears came. I *had* reached the first stages of manhood. Not long afterward, I began to smoke and drink tea—both unacceptable practices for a Mormon youth. When I once confessed this to my mother, she quietly said, "I don't believe it."

During those months in the mountains, I would ride my horse some thirty-five miles back to Blairmore. After I bought the food and packed it on the horse, there was no room for me to ride, so I walked in front. On one occasion, Tom Muckle insisted I bring back a hundred pounds of salt for the sheep, so my horse was loaded to more than full capacity. I was leading him through a break of open country, and came across another herd of sheep with two men who were taking care of them. They appeared not to believe their eyes. Who was I? Where was I going? They insisted that I stay with them over night, for it was then getting dark. They helped me unpack my horse, cooked me a nice dinner, and insisted that I sleep between them for warmth. They also cursed a little, wondering who was to blame that a boy so young was given such a job. The next morning they packed my horse and went with me for the first two or three miles. I think I will always remember the kindness they showed me.

Tom Muckle was from New Zealand, rather cold in personality, yet not outright unfriendly. Once we ran out of food. Tom wanted me to be with the sheep, so I was unable to make the trip for supplies. Our two sheep dogs had run away and we could not handle sheep without them. This was a dramatic situation. With only mutton to eat, I took a piece of string and tied it to the head of a pin. Then I bent the pin like a hook, used a grasshopper for bait, and dropped the pin and string into a nearby stream. I caught all the fish we needed. I think this variation of diet really saved us. Eventually the sheep dogs returned to our camp, so all ended well.

On the twenty-fourth of July, a day very meaningful to a boy from Utah, the anniversary of the arrival of Brigham Young and the pioneers in the Great Salt Lake Valley, it snowed more than a foot during the night. Since our tent was just an inverted V-shaped tarpaulin, the first move we made in the morning when we woke up caused the deep snow to cascade all around us. I remember how quickly we jumped up and built a fire! I also recall how unusual it was to have such a snowstorm in the middle of the summer, even at this high elevation in the Canadian Rockies.

As fall approached, we had to move the sheep to prairie country ahead of the snow storms. Father met us a few miles out of McCloud. At that time, we were trailing the sheep down a road between fields of grain. I had slipped under the fence and taken a shock of oats for my horse to eat. Father approached us on foot. I recognized him at a distance and wondered if he would scold me for stealing the grain. I recall defining my dilemma: either my horse goes hungry or I get scolded. I decided my horse had to eat. So, before father got to where I was, I had fed the horse still another bunch of grain from the field. I had just a little feeling of defiance in me. I felt inwardly prepared for whatever father might say.

He walked up, looked down at me, and I up at him. It was a tense moment for me. We had not seen each other for months. I must have looked like a vagabond. I had worn the same shirt and the same overalls all that time. The overalls were stiff with grease from wiping my hands and from cooking over an open fire. I had tried to wash my clothes two or three times, but without much success. Father sized me up and made a single comment. He said, "You need some clothes."

We loaded the sheep on cattle cars at McCloud. Then we journeyed north to Edmonton, Alberta, and thence about a hundred miles north and east to prairie country, where the sheep wintered. Father was on the cattle train with us. We rode in the caboose, sleeping on one of the benches. Before going to sleep, father talked to me for an hour or two about staying in Canada. He explained, in some detail, how sheep multiply, and how, if I stayed with them, by the time I became a man, I would have much more than any of my brothers. He put my brothers down as not having very much and never would have, but if I were to stay with the sheep, then, as an adult, I would be ahead of them. Father was quite persuasive. I was impressed he would spend so much time with me.

I wrote home to mother saying father wanted me to stay in Canada and maybe it wouldn't be such a bad idea, though I think I was not completely convinced. In any case, when mother received that letter, she went on the warpath. She communicated with each of her children, expressed her indignation, and solicited their intervention to get me home. I was told that each of them did write to my father. One of my brothers used pretty strong language. He said that if I were not home in a week, he would come and get me. He told my mother that I was too fine a boy to be left in Canada and become like he had become while he was there.

Father received these letters at his ranch in southern Alberta. He then visited us in northern Alberta. He got off the train and hired a buckboard to take him to the herd of sheep, some twenty miles from the railroad. I recall this encounter vividly. It was similar to the one that had taken place several months before. I had prepared lunch for Tom, and while he ate, I herded the grazing sheep. Father had located our camp, talked a few moments with Tom, then driven out to where I was, a mile or two away. He told me to get in the wagon. "This man will drive you to the railroad station, and here is enough money for you to get your ticket home." It was all he said. I explained that I wanted to go back to camp and get the muskrat fur cap I had purchased at the Hudson's Bay store in Edmonton on our way north with the sheep. I remember his saying, "Oh, I know. Tom said you wouldn't leave without that cap, so I put it in with your things. Now you can go back with this man." I got in the buckboard beside the driver and he took me to the railroad. The train to Utah stopped often. It was the time of the flu epidemic, so the doors of the cars were sealed whenever we stopped.

A Confrontation

Father was indeed an austere man. I never recall his arm on my shoulder or a smile for me. This is not to say that he was cruel, it was just his nature. I remember when quite young saying to my mother, "Oh, I wish I had a father." She asked me why I said that, and I replied, "Oh, I think I would like a father so I could tell him some of the things I do and some of the things I win." This must have made her quite sad. Certainly, I never had a father who seemed interested in me. He no doubt felt some responsibility, but he didn't show it. Perhaps his estrangement from my mother carried over to me.

Once when I was fifteen, I met my father in his law office in the Templeton Building. I told him quite frankly about my feelings when I had been sent to wild mountain country with only one sheepherder. I told him that I had always thought one day I would have to tell him how I felt. I said, "I am a man now and could do that kind of work. But then I was a child and I remember that once you saw me crying in my loneliness. Those months were a nightmare to me, but now I will just forget about it." It is painfully clear that I have not forgotten.

I tell about this confrontation to indicate something of the self-reliance I had developed. He said: "Now see here, I don't want a son of mine to talk to his father that way." I apologized. I told him I was sorry. It was the last time I ever saw him.

Getting Fired

Sometimes in memory and recollection, failures are ignored or neglected, but I do recall being fired on two occasions. The first time was when I was working with several other boys picking cucumbers for a pickling factory. The cucumber patch was located west of Farmington near the Great Salt Lake. One day a bird, larger than I had ever seen, landed in the middle of our patch. I was enthralled and curious. Apparently the bird had been injured because we were able to surround it and look at it closely. My curiosity kept me looking at the bird longer than appropriate for my job.

That evening as we were leaving, I was told not to come back to work again. I couldn't have been more shocked. I followed the boss as he rode his horse home, about two miles away. I simply couldn't stand the idea of losing my two dollars each day. I had never earned so much money. I ran alongside the horse, sometimes in the rear, then again alongside, begging for my job. I told him how badly I needed it. I asked him to reconsider. It wasn't until he arrived home, got off his horse, and was looking down at me that he told me I could return the next day. He explained that the owner of the pickling company had been in the field that day and had seen me wasting time looking at the bird. "He told me to fire you," my boss explained. However, he decided he would take his chances and let me stay if I were careful in the future. I must have made a very strong impression to get him to disobey his supervisor. I held the job. I guess a twelve-year-old, pleading as if it were for his life, can change a man's mind.

Another time, years later, I was fired for not following instructions in taking care of a furnace. I had to return several times before it was "convenient" for the house owner to give me my pay. Getting fired can be a painful and demeaning experience.

Summer Jobs

The summer after I returned from Canada, I tried selling door to door for Excelsis Products Company, a fledgling operation of my brother-in-law, Lynn Fairbanks. That was easily the most unpleasant job I ever had. It took so much nerve to knock on the doors of busy housewives. I had a suitcase full of sample cosmetics and cooking extracts. Though I made better than wages, I was glad when the summer was over. I might add that, with that job, I did especially well in my native Farmington. It seemed everybody bought from me. People knew I was one of Annie Clark Tanner's boys though I recall I was too proud to call at homes where my friends lived, especially if a girl friend lived there.

The next summer I was mature enough to work as a section hand on the Denver & Rio Grande Railroad. It was my first adult job with adult pay. I was fifteen but tall for my age. I bought a new and beautiful "Indian" bicycle, and rode it to the railroad toolhouse, two miles west of our home in Farmington. When I applied for the job, I was asked my age. When I started to answer, the man interrupted me, "You're twenty-one, aren't you?" The man next to him confirmed this judgment by saying something to the effect that, "Sure, he's twenty-one. You can tell that to look at him." I was glad to be employed, without too much worry about the age requirement. It was a time of a serious labor shortage.

I began this job with the speed we used on my uncle's farm. The foreman came up to me in the middle of the day and said I had better slow down if I wanted to last until six o'clock. I didn't slow down. I lasted it out. But later I paced myself better with the other men. The railroad gang comprised a Japanese foreman, immigrants newly arrived from southern Europe, and one or two men who were black. I can't remember any of the specific issues, but frequently an argument got started, or a threat with a shovel led to a fist fight. I tried to be friendly and gave in easily rather than risk a job I prized so highly. The pay was, as I remember, about three dollars a day, a huge increase over pay on the farm or house-to-house selling.

The next year, I got a similar job as a track worker on the Union Pacific Railroad. With this job, I was much nearer to my home. One day after work, all tired out, I walked slowly past the stockyard where I had once worked with my cousin, Rulon Clark. He must have noticed my fatigue and certainly the dirt on me from the railroad trains whizzing by. He spoke to me and said with friendly encouragement, "Never mind, Fanny" (a nickname he and his brothers had given me when they saw me using a broom to sweep some leaves from the walk of their home—clearly a woman's work and deserving of a girl's name), "Some day you can look back and say this job was where you got started."

Rulon sensed that I had a lot of ambition, and in return I always admired him. When he was captain of the University of Utah basketball team that won the national collegiate championship in Chicago, I milked his share of the cows.

My First Experience as an Entrepreneur

While working on the tracks of the Union Pacific Railroad, I saw, over the fence, a large field just planted in sugar beets. The farmer in me prompted my inquiry as to whether I might get a contract to thin the beets, then hoe them, later pull the weeds, and finally, in the fall, top and load them. I was successful in signing a contract with the owner of this large field, the Livingston Livestock Company. I quit my job as a railroad track worker and was back on the farm. This was my first venture as an entrepreneur.

It was shortly after starting this job that I was taken to the hospital with a serious case of appendicitis. My appendix broke while being removed and the resulting infection nearly took my life. I lost weight and after a month in the hospital was, as they said, "skin and bones." During this illness, my mother, with the help of neighbors and her grandchildren, finished the job of thinning the sugar beets. Later I was able to take over and complete the contract. That fall, to do the heavier work of topping and loading the beets, I hired grown men who were living in my neighborhood. They came to my home for their paycheck. I was an employer. I may have taken some risk when I signed the contract, but I made better than wages.

High School Days

I enjoyed my high school days. I had the leading role in the school play, and toured the state as a member of the debating team. Our principal at Davis County High School was L. J. Muir, a hero to me. He taught an English class and we read *Silas Marner,* which I greatly enjoyed. Mr. Muir told my mother I was a good English student. This may have been an exaggeration but if it had any basis it was because in our family we were encouraged to study at home. Uncle Timmy, mother's half-brother who lived alone, often took his meals with us. I think he paid some for his support. He was always interested in our studies and it became almost a sport to try to outspell him, give the best possible definition of a word, or correct some grammatical structure. I always read my English themes to Uncle Timmy and he never failed to praise me for my effort. Thus, I had encouragement in my love for writing.

During these years, I continued to work after school for my Uncle Eddy on his dairy farm. I used some of the money I earned to take dancing lessons in Salt Lake. I wanted to dance, and I didn't want to step on the girls' feet. My dancing teacher was a relative of the famous ballet teacher, Willam Christensen. I remember my mother was surprised when she learned how I was spending my money. It may be she was pleased, but of that I'm not sure.

I always took a fancy to some particular girl I thought was the very nicest. Sometimes my fascination was for a girl who didn't even know me. Frequently, I was too shy to ask for a date or even a dance. But life seemed to be made a little brighter by a special girl friend. In return, to be known as "a perfect gentlemen" was one of my enduring ambitions.

I have heard it said that happy memories are the best gift a parent can give to a child. My mother gave me many of them. I enjoyed her approval with my every accomplishment. Happy memories in my high school years were some of her gifts to me. She was pleased when I traveled for our high school debate team, entered speech contests, or participated in the school play. Everybody needs an audience, and mother was mine. In her autobiography in 1941, she wrote: "Each mother is proud of her children, and I of mine. But the real achievements are the first ones. It is not so important to count the gains of maturity."

My Life as a Carpenter

The summer I was sixteen, my older brother, Kneland, decided he could get me a good job as a carpenter on the Denver & Rio Grande Railroad. His plan wasn't quite ethical. Kneland himself applied for the job as a bridge carpenter, then gave me his railroad pass that would take me to where the job was located, and loaned me his tools. Soon I was on the train to Richfield, Utah, wondering whether I could pass as a carpenter. My only experience with tools had been making a table in a high school manual-training class. But I made it. With other workers, I lived in a boxcar on a railroad siding. Fortunately it was rough carpenter work, not requiring much skill. We repaired a water tank, fixed right-of-way gates, etc. An elderly lady cooked for us, and one day she confided to me that the foreman, E. J. Ashman, had said I was the best man on the job. To this day, that compliment pleases me.

After work, and after dinner was served in one of the bunk cars, I would go to the public library and study algebra. I intended to take algebra that fall at the University of Utah. My brother insisted this would be a good test of whether I was smart or dumb. I took the class and got on fairly well—not smart, but not dumb, so I continued to register for university classes.

While I was working inside a big water tank, near the top, my new hammer fell into the water and sank to the bottom, about twenty-five feet. The boss had gone to Salt Lake for a weekend. While he was gone, I was determined to get my hammer. I pulled the chain, the same as a fireman would use to fill the water tank of the engine. This drained all the water out of the huge container. I went down an inside ladder and got my hammer. Then I discovered that the force of so much water hitting the track below had washed out the earth and left the rails and ties without much support. I was alone, and for what seemed like a long time, I frantically shoveled dirt and gravel to make the track safe for the next train. I remember it seemed like a close call.

I had a brush with far greater danger the next summer. I hired out on the same railroad, again as a carpenter, but this time on my own. Our crew was located far out in desert country, about twenty miles southeast of Price, at Mounds, Utah. On a Sunday, when the boss went to Salt Lake, the loneliness of the weekend made some of us decide to take our rail motorcar and ride it up the tracks to Price.

The tracks in that part of the country were all curves. We were going about thirty miles an hour when we sighted a passenger train coming down the single track we were on. We slammed on the brakes and were barely able to lift one end of the car around at right angles and then roll it off the tracks before the train whizzed by. That may have been the closest call I ever had.

Swimming Races, Happy Memories, and Copper

In the summer of 1923, I applied to Utah Copper Company (now Kennecott) for a job as a carpenter. It was closer to home, in Magna, west of Salt Lake City. I was then more confident with the use of my tools. The job was building the drag classifiers used in the first step of separating the pulverized copper concentrates.

I remember my great happiness, going home to Farmington on a Saturday evening, and thence to Lagoon, the amusement park, where I would meet and dance with the girls I had made friends with in high school. I loved to dance and felt nothing but pain when the orchestra played the last tune, "Good Night, Ladies."

That summer I won the Saltair–Antelope Island swimming race. As I remember it, about fifteen people, ten men and five women, were ferried over to the south end of Antelope Island. Several boats accompanied our swim back, about five miles, all under the strict rules of the National Amateur Athletic Association. I recall that my swimming trunks were too tight and I took them off, pushing them inconspicuously into one of the boats as it passed by, then putting them back on before the finish of the race. Perhaps some rule could have penalized me, but no one complained. I was presented with a loving cup that evening during the dance intermission at Saltair.

When our children were small, they discovered the loving cup in an old trunk. Grace overheard one of them say to their young friends: "Daddy won this for swimming across the ocean." As a member of the university swimming team, my specialty was in the long distances. I always enjoyed participating in sporting events.

The next summer, 1924, I worked again at the Magna Mill of Utah Copper Company. We built the big ore dump and I was promoted to straw boss. I think I received the promotion because I suspected that one of the walls we were building was not exactly plumb. I checked it out and informed the boss of my findings. He stopped the concrete pour just in time, and we were able to get the wall on a true plumb. I felt I had become a full-fledged carpenter then, though I never thought of leaving the university to take a permanent job in that profession. It was during those summer months in Magna that I grappled with the next great decision of my life: the decision to accept a call to serve as a missionary for the Mormon church.

Chapter Three

A Mission

. . .

Chapter Three

A Mission

There is a limit where the intellect fails

and breaks down, and this limit is where the questions

concerning God, freedom, and immortality arise.

—Immanuel Kant

■ ■ ■

My mission for the LDS church greatly influenced later events in my life: the opportunity for teaching, writing textbooks, founding the O. C. Tanner Company, and even my good fortune in finding the girl I was to marry

I served my mission in what is now eastern Germany and western Poland: first in Chemnitz, Saxony; then six months in Plauen, Vogtland; and the last year in Stettin, Pomerania.

I took my work seriously, perhaps too seriously. At a tender age I took on the role of a minister of the gospel, meeting people who were discouraged, living with the tragedy of death and destruction. But perhaps the most difficult part of my mission had to do with the problems of my own religious faith. I had so many doubts and questions. In a way, it was a wonder I accepted a call to go on a mission at all. On the other hand, I had many happy experiences as a result of that decision: making new friends, forging a personal faith grounded in hope, and helping others. I seem always to have been attracted to what I thought were the best qualities of a religious life.

A Definition of Religion

My own definition of religion is based on Plato's trinity; that is, whenever anyone finds some ultimate Goodness,

Truth, or Beauty, to which one becomes committed, then one participates in religious experience. This means that the work of science, art, public life—all may be the expression of genuine religious life. This is a very broad definition, but it is the one I have come to like best. To me, the practice of goodness, the reverence for truth, and the creation or appreciation of beauty are manifestations of religious life. In such pursuits, one may become a truly religious person, and I rather doubt one can outside them.

I came to believe it is important to keep knowledge and religion together. The Mormon scriptural work, the Doctrine and Covenants, states, "the glory of God is intelligence," and while religion is a matter of faith, more than a matter of reason, still, religious faith should not contradict the world of reason. I go so far as to hope that all religious faith can be reasonable, that it can meet the test of common sense. Religion is a trust, a hope that the noblest in human life will finally be sustained. Some have described religion as an undying hope for a better world, a hope that beyond tomorrow's sunrise, a more perfect life can be achieved. Others have said, simply, that religion is the love of God and man, or that religion strives for nobility in personal character and public goodness. I like these definitions, and many others. Various expressions of religion are to be found throughout the world. I honor all of them and feel a deep sense of reverence for religious life.

My Early Religious Environment

In my early years, I was greatly influenced by my Sunday school teachers, by church leaders, and by nearly all of my relatives, especially my mother. But perhaps most of all, I was influenced by my peers. Like all youth, I wanted their approval. All these elements, together with regular attendance at church services, not to mention my love of religious music, combined to make religion a strong influence in my life.

I have a boyhood memory of playing ball in the street on a Sunday. This was not forbidden but it was frowned upon. My mother would pass by, walking on her way to church, sometimes pausing to ask, "Would you like to go to sacrament meeting with me?" Sacrament meeting was the Sunday afternoon meeting devoted to the sacrament and to preaching.

Instantly I would give up the game, and rush into the house to wash and change clothes. Mother waited for me and seemed very pleased to have me walk by her side. To please her was always a great satisfaction for me. Not so pleasing were the hard seats and long sermons. When the bishop announced the closing hymn, I felt like a bird must feel about to fly out of a cage. But I always enjoyed the organ and the singing of both choir and congregation.

Mormon children are baptized at the age of eight, and boys ordained to the lesser, or *Aaronic,* priesthood (named after Aaron, the brother of Moses) when twelve. I was made a Deacon at that age, which authorized me to pass the bread and water of the sacrament, emblems in memory of the Lord's last supper. Then I was promoted in the priesthood to the office of Teacher at fourteen. This gave me authority to go with an adult on the assignment of what was then called ward teaching. We would make informal visits to a given number of homes of church members, to teach and inquire about their welfare. No doubt this practice was important in pioneer life. Its value was to keep harmony within a religious community and offer help to those in need. At sixteen, I was made a Priest, which qualified me to consecrate the bread and water of the sacrament and to perform baptisms. Finally, I became an Elder, holding the *Melchizedek* priesthood (Melchizedek being the name of an ancient prophet whom the Mormons believe ordained Abraham), which made me eligible to go out into the world as a missionary. This was the religious pattern or structure of my early life. I recall I was sometimes given special recognitions for regular church attendance and was honored to be in the presidency of one of my priesthood quorums.

Family Freedom in a Conservative Culture

I have praised the free discussions which reigned in my mother's household. I'm sure her tolerance and encouragement helped to make her children independent and confident adults. I learned this was mother's goal. In her autobiography, she tells about the value of freedom in rearing her family. John Stuart Mill's essay "On Liberty" had a great influence on her view of a parent's role. She once told me, "That essay was my Bible."

While I was still in high school, not yet mature enough to critically judge religious beliefs and doctrines, I recall standing outside the church one evening with my bishop. He pointed to the beautiful Evening Star and with some reverence said: "Some think that star is the City of Enoch that was taken up into heaven, as told about in the Book of Mormon."

I recall I was surprised when he said this, for I had studied a little astronomy, enough for such a belief to be a shock to me. But my difficulty was not so much the improbability of a city lifted into heaven, as the suspicion I had that other things he believed and preached, might also be incompatible with common sense. But in spite of the naïveté of my bishop's faith, I was impressed with his exemplary life. Overall, my environment gave me a love for my church, and I seemed to have grown up with unbounded optimism and a cheerful disposition—perhaps in part as a result of the religious culture into which I was born.

Reasons for Accepting a Missionary Call

The transition from being a student in a university, to a full-time minister of the gospel, was a big one. As a student I was asking questions and searching for answers among the various sciences and humanities. As a missionary I was giving answers, bearing my testimony to people, and asking them to believe what I claimed to know. But giving final answers did not seem fully to conform to my personality and disposition.

At that time—and I remember pondering it hard—I thought a mission would be a time to find answers, quite as much as one finds answers in attending a university. I thought it might be an even better opportunity, since I would be immersed in full-time religious activity. It was this prospect of a total religious environment that appealed to me as the best way to discover whether the claims of my church were true. I must have done some careful thinking at that time, for I recall wondering about the possible error I might be making, that of submitting myself to a situation where the answers I sought would be predetermined. Total activity in proselyting hardly lends itself to objectivity or open inquiry. I had no answer to this difficulty. And yet I thought that such a controlled environment, for all its possible difficulties, might be a pathway to basic truths in religion, perhaps in ways I could not foresee.

Little did I realize then that religion is not primarily an intellectual affair, but involves other aspects of our human nature. The answers I found as a missionary, were answers more of the heart than of the mind. Innocently I accepted a call to serve as a missionary in order to find intellectual answers. I began a search for conclusions that I hoped would be acceptable to a critical and reflective mind. I wanted my ideas to have believability, both to myself and to others. I was naïve to expect so much.

Such expectations created a religious crisis during the first six months of my mission. I thought then, as I do now, that the strongest reason for going on a mission, should be one's own personal convictions, the desire to share one's deepest commitments. In Mormon circles, this commitment is referred to as a testimony of the Gospel. I had a moderate testimony. I was some kind of believer. Certainly I was a sincere seeker. And I was proud of my church. I could accurately say I loved the church, especially the wonderful people who belonged to it—my parents, relatives, and friends. I was a Mormon whose ancestors had joined the church in its very first years. My grandparents and great-grandparents, on both my father's and mother's sides of the family, were associated with Joseph Smith and Brigham Young. My ancestors had greatly helped their struggling church.

For many people, recalling one's ancestors can tip the scales favorably toward religious beliefs and traditions, especially when there were years of religious persecutions. Surely I was influenced by my family history and the traditions of my church. It was understandable that I would be called on a mission, but not so understandable, was my acceptance, when already I had doubts and reservations.

Prior to my mission, in the summer of 1924, I was working as a carpenter at the Magna Mill of the Utah Copper Company. I lived in a company boardinghouse and worked a ten-hour day, including Saturdays. The pay was good, but I was lonely, seeing very little of my friends or family. About my only recreational or emotional outlet was to attend church on Sunday, but even that was with some reservations. I would slip out of the church just before the sermon began. I loved the part of the religious service devoted to prayer, singing hymns, and partaking of the sacrament, but some of the sermons that followed were not quite acceptable to my thinking. I had had three years at the university and many of the ideas I absorbed in science, history, literature, and philosophy, were fresh in my mind. They influenced my acceptance or rejection of parts of the sermons preached. Sometimes my level of tolerance did not allow me to be patient. Frequently, after being inspired by the music and prayer and the quiet reflective time during the sacrament, I found that I did not want this good spirit spoiled by some of the claims made in the sermon. Mormonism is a lay-leadership church, and individual interpretations, formed and repeated uncritically, can pain the thinking man or woman.

I had reached the age of reflective thought, but also the age when religious conversion is a common experience.

I loved my church and I loved my university, and for the balance of my life I knew I would be trying to reconcile them. In those summer months, living in Magna, I had plenty of time to think about whether to go on a mission or continue with my university studies. I decided to accept the missionary call. A strong factor favoring this decision was the peer pressure, so common among young people, especially among Mormon youths. I knew I would be held in esteem by friends if found worthy to fill a mission. It may be that this peer pressure is greater than parental pressure, or even greater than one's own personal religious convictions. In any case, social considerations offered me strong incentives for missionary service, but not the strongest.

As I recall, the strongest reason for going, was the chance I felt it would give me to find answers to two questions. The first, and most important for me at that time, was whether Mormonism itself were true. The second, though nearly as important, was whether any religion were true. My college days had generated in me a fair amount of agnosticism, if not a little atheism. In any case, as Aristotle said: "Man by his very nature wants to know," and at that time I greatly wanted to know if religion were true or not true. I thought a mission was my best chance to find out, and more, I thought finding out might be important to the future of my life.

I suppose one could say I was a religious person, at least in some general sort of way. I had been raised in a religious environment. I was always searching for the highest ideal, the very best, and I came to believe that, generally, religion offered the best, the finest way to live. It was not in politics, not in school, not in business, but in religion, that I found the best expression of noble ideals. I was quite serious about life, and I wanted to discover the best and follow it, wherever it might lead.

One of the experiences that led to my accepting the mission call was a visit with Adam S. Bennion, Commissioner of Education for the LDS church. It was my first contact with a person of great distinction, and I was very grateful for it.

We talked until almost midnight in Dr. Bennion's home. He was well educated and liberal in his views.

Adam S. Bennion greatly influenced my life from the time I was about eight years old. My mother was away on a nursing case and Dr. Bennion spoke in a sacrament meeting in Farmington. I was so deeply impressed that I wrote my mother, "Adam Bennion spoke in our sacrament service today and I have decided that I want to be a teacher." My mother kept the letter and later published it in her autobiography. It may seem incredible, at least it is for me, that from that decision at eight years of age, I have never deviated. To be a teacher was my vision of the finest vocation. I never lost that dream.

I took every opportunity to hear Adam Bennion speak. For his day, he was to the Mormons what Harry Emerson Fosdick, preacher of Riverside Church in New York, was to Protestants: both were incomparable preachers. Some of the great moments in my young life were personal chats with Adam Bennion about the problems of life. He not only gave me what I thought was sound advice, but he encouraged me toward genuine liberality in the world of religion. Later he became an apostle of the LDS church.

Mother was pleased with my decision to go on a mission. I recall her saying that none of her other children had been on a mission and it would be an exceptional thing if I were to accept the call. On the other hand, one or two of my professors at the university, with whom I chanced to speak, wondered why I would want to go. Their comments gave me reason to pause. But then there were friends whose company I enjoyed, especially my girl friends. They seemed to like a young man who had filled a mission. My close friends in Farmington were accepting their calls. The people of my ward were glad when I accepted. They contributed their hard-earned pennies, nickels, or even an occasional dollar—enough money to pay my fare to the mission field in Germany.

I became involved in going through the temple and receiving my endowments (the sacred Mormon ceremonies which signify a deep commitment to the faith), and being set apart as a minister of the gospel. I accepted all this willingly and happily. Looking back, I have often reflected that I was completely free in my decision. I voluntarily chose to be a missionary for my church, however much I had to struggle for a religious faith, or however deep and profound some of my misgivings later became. This was a choice I freely made.

As a missionary, I was, for the first time in my life, identifying myself on a full-time basis with the discipline of an organization. Such a complete vocational identity was new to me. I had never felt institutional pressure before, at least not so much. In my earlier life, there had been no father to direct me, and my mother's code of honor was to give each child the greatest possible freedom. A shift from a life of almost complete personal independence, to one of close supervision by an institution—as the missionary life required—was not easy for me. I voluntarily accepted a new way of life where the daily use of personal freedom, of thought and expression, was not the pattern. Now the ideal was conformity. I understood the need for unity and loyalty, but this new emphasis on conformity was less appealing.

A memorable day in my life was October 24, 1924, when I left Salt Lake for Germany. Many friends and church members, possibly two hundred or more, were at the Union Pacific Railroad station to say farewell to thirteen of us who were leaving. I recall that quite a few of my girl friends were there and I kissed them all goodbye. After I boarded the train and reflected on these excessive romantic gestures, I had strong guilt feelings. But they soon disappeared and I was glad I had kissed all of them! One of my friends who was there insists that I kissed one girl who turned to him and asked in astonishment, "Who is that man who just kissed me?"

Anyway, I mention this excitement to explain some of the background of young Mormon people who go into the world as missionaries—the peer pressure and the adventure of it all. Those moments for me, were in sharp contrast to what was later to be the lonely environment of a missionary, away from home, in a strange city, adjusting to a different culture, with only one or two English-speaking missionary companions.

A Religious Crisis

After I had been in the mission field a few months, I experienced an emotional crisis. One might say it was a religious crisis—whether to believe or not to believe, whether to continue with my mission or go home. Such religious crises are common near the end of the teen years. Mine was critical because I was doing the work of a missionary all day long, followed by "cottage meetings," attended by those wanting to investigate Mormonism, nearly every evening.

A missionary's routine started early each morning with a meeting, which included prayer and admonitions about how to do our work, and then tracting from door to door for three hours. We spent our afternoons calling at the homes of church members and persons who indicated some interest in the church. This program for five days a week, plus meetings all day Sunday, week after week and month after month, was my life. I did not mind the intensity of the work. My problem was doubt and disbelief. My question was whether to give up my mission and return home to attend the university or to stay on this demanding schedule of work—work in whose basic message I did not believe, or believed only in part.

How, I asked myself at that time, did I ever get myself into such a painful dilemma? Should I go home and disappoint all who believed I would make a good missionary, or stay and advocate religious ideas I was myself not sure about. I thought I had already solved this problem when I decided to go on a mission. But I hadn't. I had not realized the depth of my doubting. Nor had I had any experience with the discipline demanded of a missionary, a discipline which ran counter to my disposition of curiosity and exploration.

In those first six months as a missionary, I worked very hard. At the time, I recall thinking that I outworked any of my missionary companions. I was hoping my doubts would resolve themselves. They didn't. Instead, things grew worse. I prayed, rather feebly, about my lack of faith, but got no answer. I marshaled all the arguments I could that would justify my resigning from my mission, balancing those against the arguments favorable to my continuation. What I decided to do was important to me. I was a serious judge of myself, possibly too serious, possibly too self-critical.

As tension grew within me, I disclosed my disbeliefs to my missionary companion, Horace Kunz. Then I revealed these doubts in a missionary testimony meeting where about twenty missionaries were present. As they listened, they were quiet, but afterwards were still very friendly, something that surprised me at the time. I felt like a deserter. I must have feared they would disown me. They were not even argumentative, as I expected they would be.

Then, later, in a larger meeting of missionaries attended by Apostle James E. Talmage, president of the European Mission, I decided the moment of truth had come. With some emotion, and with what I thought was clear reasoning, I told them that because of my doubts and outright disbeliefs, I should quit the mission field and go home. Then I added that the only reason for not doing so, was my lack of personal courage. I hated to face my family and friends with such a failure. In my talk, I recall mentioning a friend at home who believed in me, an old man, J. D. Wood, who despite his modest circumstances, had pressed a five-dollar bill in my hand when I went to tell him goodbye. His sacrifice was vivid in my memory. I would have to face him with my failure.

The missionary meeting, with such a confession of personal doubt, was charged with emotion, more of my own, no doubt, than of others present. I was surprised at the response. I expected President Talmage to accept my resignation. Instead, when he got up to speak he was gentle and, I thought, quite reflective. He talked of reasons for our discouragement, even including our temptations from the devil (whose existence I doubted). After the meeting he asked me to go for a walk with him. He praised me for my intellect and went so far as to predict I would yet fill a great and important mission. I was impressed with what he said, but also greatly surprised. The result was that I decided to remain in the mission field for a time, and think more carefully about whether to go home.

Four Questions

As I reflected on my situation at that time, there were four specific issues that challenged my faith in Mormonism. There may have been other grounds for my doubts, but I recall the urgency of these four.

First, I read and reread several times one particular tract I was to pass out for people to read, entitled "Can All Churches Be From God?" The more I read, the more I disagreed. I was sure that all churches *could* be from God if they helped people. The author of the tract argued otherwise. The Mormon church was God's only way to salvation. There were other doctrinal claims with which I disagreed. But here was a major difference I had with my church, a difference about a single road to salvation. This difference remains with me to this day.

The second doubt seemed a heresy far deeper, I thought, than any I had about Mormon doctrine, for it called into question the basis for any belief in the Christian or any other religion. On one occasion, when I knocked on a door to give a tract, an elderly woman answered. I told her I was a missionary for my church, the Church of Jesus Christ of Latter-day Saints. She drew herself up with some defiance, and told me a tragic story.

"God?" she asked, "Christ? I once believed what you are saying. But I do not believe it any more. First, I lost my husband in the war. (World War I was then very recent history.) Then I lost my two sons in the war; then my daughter. Now I am alone. We had a beautiful home, now this poverty and loneliness! I don't believe a word you are saying about God, that he loves and Jesus will save us. Here, take your tract and go away and do not come back!"

I was silenced. My message seemed a hollow one. I recall afterward, sitting alone in a public park, trying to read a book that would give me answers to what she had said. It didn't help. I felt keenly sympathetic with the plight of the woman I had just met, and I have never forgotten her disbelief. She is always vaguely present to shade some of the sunshine of a positive and confident religious faith. Through her I had met the problem of evil and suffering, the greatest challenge to all religious faith. Emotionally, I wanted my mission to help people, but could I reason away the doubts and problems some people face? To say that the answer is not within the bounds of human reason, but lies in religious faith, when such a faith blinks at the cruel facts of life, will this do? I wondered. I could not find satisfactory answers. My religious thinking was suffering a baptism in the harsh realities of human existence.

My third basis for doubt was the account I eagerly read of the Scopes trial in Tennessee. Mother subscribed to several magazines for me, some of which I requested. One of them was *Current History*. It devoted a whole issue to the Scopes trial. I had come to accept evolution from three years of study at the university. But now I was immersed in a religious environment that affirmed belief in God's special creation. I had difficulty reconciling this notion with my sense that eons of time were required for the earth to reach its present condition; that there was no special design, just survival of the fittest; that billions of species had finally become extinct. Evolution seemed simply one of the overwhelming conditions of all life on this planet earth. How did God fit in to this chaotic scheme?

A fourth cause of my doubting came from reading an account of the first years of the church in Joseph Fielding Smith's unabridged history, which one of the other missionaries had brought with him. It was clear, at least to me, that Mormonism had an origin quite as natural as the beginning of any organization. Yet somehow the assumption was made of an incredible amount of supernatural intervention. "Thus sayeth the Lord" introduced the solution of too many of the founders' daily problems.

With these four reasons for questioning—whether there be only one true church, the problem of evil and suffering, issues raised by the theory of evolution, and the all-too-human elements in the founding of Mormonism—I had a battle on my hands, a struggle with doubts of major proportions. In the background of these arguments was the constant awareness of friends and relatives back home. I still did not want to disappoint them.

The crisis I went through at that time was much deeper than the issue of the Mormon church versus other churches. The issues for me were: Is there a God? Can I accept any of the churches? Does the whole creation have any meaning? If so, what is that meaning? What is humanity's ultimate destiny?

Some Answers

I finally came to see that such questions were beyond the reach of my past studies in the university, though I still felt sure academia would have important things to say about any and every subject. I finally concluded that whatever answers there may be to these basic questions, faith would still be required; one would have to go beyond the evidence. But then, I asked, what to believe, even on faith? Where to start?

I recall reading one man's desperate reach for something to believe. He said his starting place was this: "I believe in the ultimate decency of things, and if I awoke in hell, I would still believe it." Such a basic faith impressed me. Maybe I could adopt it as a beginning for my own faith. If only there were a "decency in things," the world's existence would be justified. I did not want to believe that the whole creation is just billions of atoms going at it blindly. But as a missionary I needed more—religious beliefs that I could preach about.

My search for convictions I could defend and advocate, resulted in an experience of religious conversion. It happened this way: I was riding on a streetcar, reading a religious book that had a statement something like this: "When men rise to their best, they but say 'Amen' to the life and teachings of Christ." I was stirred with a strong emotion that compelled me to respond favorably to this statement. If this is true, I thought, then I will study the life and teachings of Christ.

So, leaving aside the unique teachings of my own church, I decided I would first study the religion of Christianity. I was reading articles in *Catholic World,* the *Christian Century*, and several other publications. Also, as time would allow, I read a number of books on religion—James E. Talmage's *Articles of Faith* that explained the Mormon religion, and books written by Harry Emerson Fosdick. In later years, Dr. Fosdick became a hero to me and a major influence in my life. When I was a student at Harvard, I regularly listened on the radio to his Sunday sermons from Riverside Church. Once he came to Harvard to preach in Appleton Chapel, and I got a seat as near the pulpit as I could. His subject for that Sunday was: "Are Religious People Fooling Themselves?" I recall that a couple who must have been observing my intense interest invited me to dinner in their home. My hero-worship for Dr. Fosdick must have been quite apparent to them.

The Foundations for My Religious Faith

In any case, my religious experience told me that faith in the life and teachings of Christ was the foundation I had been seeking. With this as my base, I began to discover convictions I could talk and preach about. Such a faith, of course, would involve the teachings of my own church, particularly those teachings that appealed to me personally: the doctrine of eternal progression, the view that individuals continue to grow and learn throughout eternity; the idea of Mormonism as a restored Christianity; and the overall philosophy of Mormonism as a way of life, particularly as taught by Christ and our church leaders.

My personal crisis issued finally in deep convictions, a sense of meaning, new energy. I came to love people, all kinds of people, and try to influence them for good, all who would take time to listen to me. I decided I would postpone or put on the shelf, for later consideration, the unanswered questions I was concerned about. Now I had missionary work to do, assignments to complete. I wanted to do this work to the best of my ability.

The crisis was over, but I still had to work out what to teach and preach. I concluded that the core of a religious faith should be practical—to love and help people. To this ideal I gave my total commitment. Soon I was back to my youthful and cheerful religious ways of thinking and doing. I still had to work through the issues every day—whether there is a God, whether God is available to help people, whether what I was doing would be significant to God—but my optimism took over. Prayer for me now became meaningful and helpful. In prayer I felt I was far along in solving the problems of my mission.

Christ as My Ideal

The basis for my religious faith now became the life and teachings of Jesus Christ. Here the emphasis would be practical, Christianity as a way of life. Jesus of Nazareth became a searchlight on problems—of family, neighbors, business, and all of society, including the problem of peace for all nations.

The ethic of love is by no means an easy standard to live by but it is *there*; it is real. Like others, I think of Jesus as the Galilean Carpenter, the hound of heaven that will not let me go. I like to think he is a companion of the way, sometimes forgotten, always neglected, yet never failing to return when life is difficult. In the competitive struggle for bread, for international goodwill, the spirit of Jesus is available to us.

I remember one of the few occasions I took the time to see a movie while on my mission. It was one of the early silent versions of *Ben Hur*. At the end, as it showed Christ on the cross between the two thieves, the last words spoken by Ben Hur were, "He is not dead, but will live in the hearts of men." I was moved by that statement. Christ had lived in the hearts of people for nearly two thousand years and lived in me also. The drama was a moving religious experience for me.

Having a basis of faith in God, in prayer, and in Christ, I began to identify these with the teachings of my church. There were other teachings I thought less important. For example, I did not preach much about the Word of Wisdom, the Mormon code of health which prohibits the use of tobacco and alcohol, among other things. This was important as a way of living, but other teachings were of greater importance. Everyone finds some particular emphasis. For myself, I tried to emphasize the teachings which addressed the great personal and social problems of that time. For example, finding a good moral and intellectual balance, a positive attitude about one's self and toward other people—all kinds of people. These were the major concerns of my mission. I came to believe in people. The members of my church became lasting friends. These friendships have endured up to the present time.

My mission was not an academic sort of experience. It was not a student affair. It was the very ultimate of meeting life head-on, dealing with the crucial problems of human existence—birth and death, war and peace, faith and despair. I worked in Germany during the worst time of inflation. In some places, food was not available. It seemed every home had a picture on the wall of a husband or son, or both, lost in the war. In such an atmosphere of despair and frustration, I preached the gospel of hope and goodwill, turning the people's thoughts from the tragedies of the past, from the grimness of the present, to hope for the future. At times, when I faced such stark realities, I felt my mission aged me considerably. Certainly I sacrificed some of the lightheartedness of a young man in his early years of maturity. I identified with the troubles of people and usually went to bed with many of their cares on my mind. I was always glad if, in their illness or despair, they asked me to pray with them. It seemed to help me as much as it may have helped them.

How did my mission change my ideas? Well, I became a converted Christian. I was totally committed as a follower of Jesus Christ, though I suppose I was more a pragmatic Christian than a theological believer. With every doctrine I put this question: If true, so what? The "so what" part was my sense that doctrines should have implications for life, should help in solving problems. One can imagine that with such convictions, much of typical religious discussion and preaching were not very relevant or interesting to me. I did not want to reduce religion to ethics; the mystery of life was too great for that. But I did want to improve the quality of human life, the "abundant life," for which Christ said he had come into the world.

Annie Clark Tanner

Joseph Marion Tanner

A teenage Obert on horseback in Canada.

Obert (third from right) with one of his railroad crews.

Young Obert in a baseball stance, at the age of fourteen.

Grace Adams Tanner, near the time of her marriage.

Obert Clark Tanner, missionary.

Dean Obert

Joan

Gordon Adams

Carolyn

Stephen Clark

David Obert

Obert and Grace at their East Millcreek home.

Chapter Four

GRACE, CHILDREN, AND FRIENDS

. . .

Chapter Four

GRACE, CHILDREN, AND FRIENDS

. . . then these things—the attachment of a few friends,

the love of a child, a wife, a brother—are seen as goods more

abiding and more satisfying than all others.

—W. T. Stace

■ ■ ■

Of all the adventures in life, I think none compares to the adventure of marriage and raising children. It can become the most precious part of one's life, and conversely, as LDS church President David O. McKay said, "No other success can compensate for failure in the home." Finding and making good friends who can endure throughout one's lifetime is another source of abiding satisfaction.

Grace Adams and I were married on August 5, 1931. We were fortunate to have six children: Dean, Joan, Gordon, Carolyn, Steven, and David. Our lives have been devoted to our family, to our three surviving children, Joan, Carolyn, and David, and seven grandchildren. We are proud of our grand-children—our daughter Joan's three sons, Patrick, Jonathan, and Christopher, and our Carolyn's four children, two sons, Stephen and Thomas, and two daughters, Jessica and Emily.

I first met Grace in June of 1927. We had a date for a Friar's Dance, sponsored by a University of Utah campus orga-nization for returned missionaries. I had just returned from my mission and, on that date, I was enthusiastically greeting old friends and former missionary companions. The occasion turned out to be the worst possible place to take a girl on a first date. She felt ignored, and, therefore, when I asked her for another date, she was busy.

We did not meet again for nearly four years. But that next meeting was about the most memorable event in my life. I think I recall every detail. It happened this way: To pay my way to attend the University of Utah and also repay the money borrowed for my mission and trip afterwards, I traveled to different high schools throughout the state, selling class rings to graduating seniors (more about that in chapter 7). I stopped in Parowan on a selling trip, and went to call on Ray Adams, Grace's brother, a favorite missionary companion in Germany. I assumed that Grace had long since married or had forgotten me.

I knocked on the Adams' front door. It was a screen door, and didn't fit too well. As I knocked, it would close and open and close again, making a noise. I waited for what seemed like a long time. Then the door opened and a beautiful girl came out. I can see her now. She had auburn hair, blue eyes, a few attractive freckles, and an especially charming smile. I remember too, her warm and friendly handclasp. She asked, "This is Obert, isn't it?"

I was delighted with her charming appearance, but I was frankly uncertain as to whether this was Grace. I started to reciprocate, "This is . . . " but I was too unsure. She didn't help me either. I must have learned already that it is bad business to call a girl by another girl's name. She seemed to enjoy waiting to see if I remembered, so I plunged in with my best guess. "This is Grace, isn't it?" It was, and I was so relieved, and pleased.

From that moment, we have enjoyed a great companionship. That evening I took Grace to the opening dance of the Mutual Improvement Association, the church organization for young people, gladly paying the annual dues of fifty cents. I had a good time, a very pleasing and happy time. We danced nearly every dance together. On my way back to Salt Lake City,

I remember saying to a friend, "I think I will marry that girl." It was an egotistical comment. When I arrived home, I told my mother I thought I had met "the future Mrs. Obert C. Tanner." I sent candy and presents to Parowan, and found excuses to return to southern Utah—such as that I needed to deliver class rings—in order to see her.

Like all courtships, ours carries tender memories. On one date we went to New Harmony, a very small town where Grace's mother was born. We visited the cemetery and found Grace's grandmother's grave in disrepair, covered with weeds. We cleaned it up and straightened the headstone. That small graveyard told me Grace belonged to the beautiful southern Utah country. Her pioneer roots were there and I liked that. It meant a lot to me. I met Grace's parents, Thomas and Luella Adams. I found them to be wonderful people.

On another date I took Grace for a swim in the hot springs near Hurricane. When I got back to Salt Lake I was telling one of my close friends about my date with Grace, about how we seemed to be so compatible, and I stressed the intellectual nature of our relationship. He was skeptical, given that she was such a pretty girl.

"You mention the intellectual, but what about the physical side?"

"Oh, that is important," I replied, "but mainly we like each other for intellectual reasons." This was too much for him.

"You mean you didn't notice her figure?" he persisted.

"Oh, yes, we went swimming together."

"And then did you notice?" he asked.

"Yes, she walked in front of me." My friend won his point.

In the spring my intentions to propose were firm. Just before Grace was to graduate from the College of Southern Utah (now Southern Utah University), I telephoned her and asked if I could take her to the graduation dance. Grace said she already had a date. I weakly replied that I guessed she probably couldn't see me on the following weekend either. Grace confirmed my fears. I wondered if I were failing to get a message about our relationship, so I made up my mind that it was time to find out.

I decided not to risk another negative answer by telephone, but to go to Parowan and confront her in person. I composed a telegram to her as follows: "I will arrive in Cedar City tomorrow at 2:00 P.M.—meet the train." This was an imperious male position, but I was in love and desperate to find out if I had a chance. When Grace met the train, she was wearing a large brimmed hat. We walked up the canyon just east of Cedar City. I kept wondering how a boy could kiss a girl with a hat like that. We came to the bank of a small creek; I held out my hand to help her. As she jumped over the stream toward me, I put my arm around her and she tilted her face, raising the brim of her hat. That kiss, I felt, sealed our fate. On the next date I had a diamond ring, which I gave her as we sat on the rim of Cedar Breaks.

We set our wedding date, August 5, 1931. The ceremony was to be in the Salt Lake Temple. I loved that beautiful building, and was pleased and proud to be married there. My uncle, Joseph Clark, one of my mother's favorite brothers, who had baptized me in the Lagoon boat pond when I was eight years old, performed the marriage ceremony. They say a boy ages with the responsibilities he assumes on his wedding day. Not so with me. On that day, I was confident, happy, and ready to face life with the one I loved so much.

Grace and I went on a honeymoon to the Canadian Rockies, Seattle, Los Angeles, and back to Salt Lake City. Our first home was near the University of Utah, where Grace registered for classes. While receiving all *A*s in her classes, she continued to keep house and cook meals that were, to me, one delightful surprise after another. Two years later we had our first baby, our boy Dean, who had the same auburn hair as his mother. All of our children had Grace's hair, except our daughter Carolyn's was slightly darker. As a small child, she told people she had "black sheep hair."

Partnership

Grace and I have maintained a partnership in our marriage. In the beginning Grace seemed to think that I knew everything. But now it is clear to her—as it is becoming clearer to me—that I know less and less and she knows more and more. So the scales are finally balancing in her favor. Nevertheless, our team has pulled together, each of us doing our share—she in making a wonderful home, and I in providing for the family. When we have had differences, we generally cleared up everything with just two words, "I'm sorry."

We have been married sixty-two years. I like to think our marriage has been a combination of romance and reason, a great love mixed with thoughtful consideration for each other. I know the number of years one is married does not, of itself, signify happiness. Still, I believe life's greatest promise of happiness lies in the love between a man, a woman, and the children they choose to bring into the world. To raise independent children and, if you are lucky, to see them happily married, with children of their own is a wonderful hope.

My friends like to invoke Martin Luther when they say, "Obert has been saved by Grace alone"—and I heartily agree with them. In later years I have tried to make up for some of my earlier chauvinism. In philanthropies, Grace's name is nearly always mentioned with my own. She has helped to make our material success and now shares a deserved recognition.

Today, in 1993, Grace and I are alone, looking after one another as we were in the beginning. We are now more thankful for each other, certainly wiser, and always glad for our companionship. I have said we tried not to over-ask of life, but we did. We couldn't help it.

Children

Grace and I are more humble now about how to raise a family. We thought we knew a great deal at the beginning. My philosophy, echoing my mother's, was to give each child as much freedom as possible, and also, at the same time, as much encouragement as possible. We felt encouragement was better than a "law and order" family. I loved my own freedom, and wanted the same for our children. When facing a challenge or confrontation, parents cannot help trying to make their children copies of themselves. Perhaps because of this inevitable tension, I cast my lot on the side of freedom for the child, as much freedom as is reasonable, whatever the results may be.

I could write many pages about our children, Joan with her art and books, and Carolyn with universities and the ministry. Both of them have wonderful families. David married Linda Murdock in August 1993. She is a lovely person. He is a wonderful son. We are very proud of both of them.

We are a family of great love and affection. In earlier years, when all our children were with us, we frequently had lawn parties, and visited the ocean or the mountains, wherever we lived. I told the children stories at bedtime—stories about my dog, Tosh; about meeting tramps on the nearby railroad, those who called at my mother's home for something to eat; about accidents I had experienced; and so on. Finally our children became old enough to suspect that what they once believed were facts, were products of my imagination.

In the summer of 1942, I was teaching at Stanford. I loved my work. We lived in a beautiful home on Waverly Street in Palo Alto. I recall so vividly how fortunate I was at that time to be the father of five children. The oldest was our son, Dean, then ten years old, and the youngest Steven, six months old. I cannot overstate how happy we all were. Grace was an ideal mother. I played with the children at every opportunity, including our good times on the beach at Half Moon Bay on Sunday afternoons, or picnicking under a huge oak tree in one of the large fields near Stanford.

Another child, Donald Tanner, my brother LaVinz's boy, became an important part of our family. Donald's mother, Phyl-

lis, died tragically when he was just a few days old. There were
four children that survived, Doris, Rex, Marion, and the baby,
Donald. Our part was to raise Donald. First, my mother took
him, for at that time I was not married. Then Grace and I
helped, and for several years he told his friends that I was his
father. Later he lived with my sister, Lois, while attending
medical school at Stanford, where he was graduated, youngest
in his class. He has been greatly loved and admired by all of us.
My two daughters, Joan and Carolyn, have a special affection
for him. Now he has a wonderful family of his own.

Tragedy

One day Dean complained of a sore throat. A woman
doctor from the Palo Alto Clinic came. She was the grand-
daughter of Dr. Ray Lyman Wilber, who was a former president of Stanford University. Within a day or two Dean's illness
was diagnosed as poliomyelitis. I rushed him in my car to the
Children's Hospital in San Francisco. In two days he was gone.

My grief was quite unbearable. I loved him so much, my
firstborn, and he loved me as only a ten-year-old boy can adore
his father. After his death I thought the world would end. His
funeral service was held in the Stanford Memorial Church,
where I was assistant to the chaplain, Elton Trueblood.

Another tragedy followed in December 1949 after we
had moved back to Utah. Grace and I had taken our four children to Brighton for a day of skiing. The youngest, Steven,
almost seven years old, took his sled. While he was on the sled
a car ran over him and killed him instantly. Grace was by his
side when it happened. I came on the scene a few moments
later. I was about out of my mind as I screamed, "Who killed
my son?" It was a young student from South America, unac-
customed to driving a car in the snow.

My dearest friends, David O. McKay and Adam S. Bennion,
were the speakers at Steven's funeral, and I recall my feeling

that this was my own funeral, for I felt I would never recover. Our other children were old enough to be deeply affected by this second death.

Our third loss occurred in May 1955. Grace and I were entertaining a history club in our home. The telephone rang and a police officer informed me that our son, Gordon, was at the County Emergency Hospital. "Don't rush your driving as he is not serious," he cautioned. We did rush and were there shortly before he died.

Gordon was seventeen years old, a junior in high school, a member of the football team and a cappella choir, class poet, honor student, and a favorite of his English teacher. He had gone up the canyon with some classmates on a yearbook-signing party. He accepted a ride home early so he could get a paper written for the next day. The boy driving turned a curve and hit a tree on the side where Gordon was sitting.

The almost unbearable sorrow of our lives is that we lost half our children. I am still stunned by the extent of such a loss. It is small comfort, but I glean some joy in the memories of our happiness with those we enjoyed so much before we lost them. Grace and I try not to live in sorrow and despair. We fill our lives with the joy of our three surviving children. I mention the deaths in our family only because my story cannot be told without them. I do it reluctantly, and only in a whisper.

Sometimes a close friend will mention our courage in living. I recall how in previous years, beginning during my mission experience, I had reasoned through the various ways people may overcome adversity. I thought I had rationalized a meaningful universe and reconciled it with tragedy and suffering. These arguments now paled before the deep sadness Grace and I endured. There was nothing to do but simply continue to live as best we could. I had no reasoning to help me; it was just go on living. As one has said: "The greater the sorrow, the less tongue it hath." I was silenced. Only now, after many years, can I write these few lines about our three sons.

Special Friends

We have been fortunate to have wonderful friends. Some of our friends have been distinguished, and some quite like ourselves. We admired all of them for their personal qualities. Some were in the academic world, some in business, and some in public life. We bear deep affection for all our friends. Here, I mention only a few of those we have known.

I traveled widely with Mrs. Eleanor Roosevelt on behalf of the United Nations organization. I shared a close friendship with former Chief Justice Warren E. Burger and served with him on the Commission on the Bicentennial of the United States Constitution. Grace and I and our family were dear friends of Professor C. I. Lewis of Harvard University and his wife, Mabel. I have already mentioned my two closest friends in the LDS church, David O. McKay and Adam S. Bennion.

Others very special to me in my journey are: Scott Matheson, Sr.; Sterling McMurrin; Lynn Bennion; Daryl Chase; Alvin Gittins; and Sister Ann Josephine.

Scott Matheson and I had the good sense and the good fortune to have married two of the Adams sisters from Parowan. Grace and her sister, Adele, were especially close. I recall how often Grace and I stopped at the home of Scott and Adele Matheson en route home from the city. Scott's good humor and brilliant mind were, I thought, unmatched. Adele was one of our dearest companions. Her son, Scott Matheson, Jr., became governor of Utah. Alice, Carol, and Bea, Grace's other sisters, also brought music and companionship to our home. Carol has been like one of our family. We enjoy her cheerful disposition. Always we were pleased when she could go with us on a trip. Her son, Bill Wright, was also dear to us. He recently passed away and we miss him.

Our friendship with Sterling M. McMurrin and his wife, Natalie, goes back over fifty years. We first met in Richfield, Utah, where he was teaching in the LDS seminary. We met again when I was teaching at Stanford. Later he became widely known in the field of education. President John F. Kennedy appointed him United States Commissioner of Education. Then Sterling served the University of Utah in various positions—as provost, vice president, and dean of the graduate school. I am very proud of his achievements in the field of the history of philosophy. We have spent many happy evenings together.

The foreword to this volume was written by M. Lynn Bennion, former superintendent of the Salt Lake City Schools. He and I rode horses together and talked for hours about education and religion. He was also formerly a supervisor of LDS seminaries. I regard him as one of the wisest persons I ever came to know. We did a lot of reconciling about philosophy and religion.

Sometimes a friend overpraises another friend. On our golden wedding anniversary, my good friend, Daryl Chase, former president of Utah State University, said of me, "Obert is the most intellectually honest person I ever met." I was honored. I recall thinking to myself that such a compliment can have a price, for it can be lonely to be honest. I doubt if any friend has better solved the historical and philosophical problems of our Mormon culture than Daryl Chase, however. He faced up to contrasts and contradictions, but always with appreciation for the best in people. He was full of hope for a better future. We shared some of our social loneliness and some of our optimism.

Another dear friend was Alvin Gittins, a genius as a portrait painter. He once told me that one of his best portraits is that of Grace. It hangs in the Alumni House at the University of Utah. I doubt if any two people enjoyed conversations more than Alvin and Grace. We enjoyed the stories he told of people whose portraits he had painted. Grace and I were greatly blessed by our friendship with Alvin and Gwen Gittins.

No doubt friendships we make have many points of attraction—good humor, common experience, a sense of shared likes and dislikes. I had an unusual friendship with Sister Ann Josephine of the Holy Cross Hospital. We met in a hospital in the context of my own suffering and loneliness. For me her friendship remains tender and strong. She is one with whom I share the deep values and mysteries of Christian faith.

Special friends were made when the Tanner Lectures were created. Among them were Lord Eric Ashby and Lady Helen Ashby of Cambridge University, England; Herbert and Jennifer Hart of Oxford University, England; Derek and Sissela Bok of Harvard University; Harold and Vivian Shapiro of Princeton University; Anthony and Belle Low of Cambridge University, England; and Jim and Anne Duderstadt of the University of Michigan. Dear friends of old who joined in this enterprise included Met Wilson, emeritus president of two universities and head of Stanford Behavioral Sciences, and his wife, Marian; David Gardner, president of the University of California, and his lovely wife, Libby, who passed away in February 1991; and Chase and Grethe Peterson of the University of Utah. My journey has been made glad by friends, those mentioned, and countless others we have dearly loved.

Our First Homes

During the first fourteen years of our married life, Grace and I lived in twenty different apartments and houses. I didn't want to buy a house. I wanted to be free to work at different universities and to pursue business opportunities. With my tendency to exaggeration, I have sometimes said to my friends that Grace and I came to live on nearly every street in Palo Alto. Our first home there was in the Barron Park area. We rented a small furnished house for $27.50 per month. Our daughter, Joan, was born in the Palo Alto Hospital, which we like to call "the hospital in the trees."

When we made our final return to Salt Lake City in 1944, we bought the first house we owned, and have lived there since, now nearly fifty years. We call this place "3501," or as Grace says "home-home." Also, we have a river home we enjoy in the summer, located in the Uinta Mountains, and a winter home located in Palm Springs, California.

Land around our Salt Lake home borders beautiful East Millcreek. We have a garden, and fruit trees, and a fountain, the first I ever built. Over the years, our children and grandchildren have enjoyed our home. Neighborhood children still come to play on our swings and slides. Once we found a note on our door from Sterling McMurrin that read: "Sorry I missed seeing you but I did count forty-seven children on your front lawn." In the summer evenings, Grace and I continue to sit in our garden, under our own fig tree, and count our many blessings. Today, in summer, we place a sign on our gates: "Visitors welcome this Sunday." People love to walk along our part of East Millcreek and enjoy the stream, flowers, and so many trees, scrub oaks, and evergreens.

One evening, as we were having dinner with some people of my company at the Salt Lake Country Club, a waitress called me to the telephone. The woman's voice on the other end of the line said:

"Mr. Tanner, do you have a home in Woodland?"

"Yes, I have," I replied.

"I regret to tell you it has burned down," she said.

"But that can't be, the building is all steel and glass."

"Mr. Tanner, I am sorry but it is burning now."

I remonstrated that the building could not burn. She offered emphatically, "Mr. Tanner, the whole horizon is red." Then I understood.

I went back to the table and said nothing until after dinner. I spoke to one or two of my executives, who got in a car and went to our newly finished home, now so completely destroyed. Some lumber had been stacked over a floor heater which the workmen had left on. This lumber caught fire. The heater fan was also on, so there was a wind that fanned the flame of the burning boards, igniting the interior of the house. Altogether, it made an enormous fire and the heat was so intense that the steel girders and steel crossbeams were twisted like spaghetti. Beneath them nothing was left but a pile of ashes. When I saw the ruins, I was truly discouraged, but we set to work as soon as possible and it was soon built again. We have subsequently enjoyed this retreat on the Upper Provo River.

Our home in Palm Springs consists of two buildings in the Blue Skies Village. There is a fountain, along with many flowers and a cactus garden. We have enjoyed this home for the past thirty years. Grace remains there during the winter months and I go back and forth to my business in Salt Lake.

A Tribute

Grace and I have had much joy together with our family and friends. We try to walk on the sunny side of the street, hurting no one and helping as opportunities come to us. We claim no more than to be average, a little better if possible, and very human withal. Aristotle says that happiness is not something attained by direct assault. Rather, happiness is a byproduct of a life fully engaged in good causes. Notwithstanding our losses, Grace and I have enjoyed our work, living each day to accomplish our goals. The following is a note I received from her on Christmas Eve 1987.

> My Dearest One,
>
> For many years you have given me great joy and loving care. Together we have shared sorrows. Without your constant strength and support I think I could not have survived. For your kindness, your strength, your optimism, your tolerance, your

generosity, your love of mankind—I salute you. In these twilight years, as we go on together, I give you my constant love and devotion.

My grateful thanks.

Yours Only,
Grace

I would like to pay a special tribute to Grace. She gave me great freedom to pursue my life's vocations. Encouraging me to do what I wanted, in teaching, business, and service to church and community, her support was strong and constant. I needed the cheerfulness and encouragement Grace gave me. Without her, my life could not have been a journey in search of freedom.

Chapter Five

WRITING

. . .

Chapter Five

WRITING

The better the book the more room for the reader.

—Holbrook Jackson

■ ■ ■

Writing has been an important part of life. My mission for the LDS church left me with a lasting interest in the New Testament. Much of my writing is responsive to it.

Teaching Seminary

After I was released from my mission, I traveled with a missionary companion for five months through the Balkans to Turkey, Palestine, Egypt, and back to Greece, Italy, and western Europe. We returned to New York, visited Washington, D.C., and then traveled to points of interest in early Mormon church history.

Having assumed a debt for this travel, I needed to secure a job as soon as possible. I applied to Dr. Adam S. Bennion, supervisor of LDS seminaries, for a teaching position. He remembered my visit with him before my mission and had sent me a book in Germany. So when I applied, he seemed pleased, and offered me an excellent position in Spanish Fork, Utah. It is important to note that nearly all active LDS young people enroll in seminary classes through their local organizations. I would be teaching religious principles to junior high and high school students and so my appointment had to be sanctioned by the local stake president (a *stake* corresponds roughly to a Catholic diocese, as a *ward* is analogous to a parish). Dr. Bennion's secretary, Mr. Davis, drove me to Spanish Fork to meet President Henry Gardner, who was also president of the local bank. We met in the bank office, and when Mr. Davis made the introduction Mr. Gardner looked me over rather sternly and, I thought, with a little disappointment. Mr. Davis did not have very much to say about me except that I had just returned from a mission to Germany.

The previous seminary teacher in Spanish Fork, Lars Eggertsen, had been a distinguished educator, a former superintendent of schools in Provo and otherwise widely known in Utah County. Mr. Eggertsen was certainly a contrast to a young man twenty-two years old, and this may have explained Mr. Gardner's dismay. Whatever reasons he had, I was a little disturbed that he was not more friendly, and so assumed a standoffish air. For a brief period I thought I might not become a teacher.

It was clear that Mr. Gardner thought of me as one of several applicants they were considering. Mr. Davis was a little put out with President Gardner for not accepting me immediately. I could see that a showdown might occur since I did not think the superintendent of seminaries would have sent me down from Salt Lake without a pretty clear understanding that I already had the job. I remained silent during their conversation. Finally, Mr. Gardner said rather emphatically that my application would be considered, and that he would have a meeting with his two stake counselors in a few days and let Adam Bennion know their decision. I could see Mr. Davis was not about to allow this conclusion, and then he said something that I remember quite well. "President Gardner, Adam S. Bennion will relieve you of any responsibility for the appointment of a teacher here in the seminary. Brother Tanner will be here in September to take up his responsibilities as principal."

Mr. Gardner was silent for a few moments and then said, "I guess if that's the way it's going to be, that is the way it will be." With that our interview ended. Looking back, I can't blame Mr. Gardner very much. My youthful appearance must have worried him.

In the year that followed, I thoroughly enjoyed my teaching. I loved the students, gave them personal attention, and I spent a lot of time in preparation for my classes. I enjoyed the people in the community, and withal, it was one of the outstanding years of my teaching experience.

During this year in Spanish Fork, we had an eminent seminary supervisor, George H. Brimhall, who was a former president of Brigham Young University. He was then an older man, approaching, I would guess, about eighty. His disposition at times could be a little impatient, and he was easily disturbed if something did not please him. I learned this when he taught a class I attended the previous summer at BYU's Alpine Summer School in Provo Canyon. The class was composed of seminary teachers and he made it clear that when he visited us in our places of employment he would have certain standards for us to meet. I remembered the standards he mentioned, and I was rather careful to live up to them.

When Dr. Brimhall came to visit me near the middle of the school year. I started to introduce him to my class, but he interrupted me rather bluntly and said, "I'll take over here. I'd like to ask the students some questions." This was said in a rather overbearing manner, and I immediately began to feel resentment.

He asked the students: "First, how many have your Bibles?" All the hands in the class went up. Then he asked several questions about parts of the Bible that we had not yet studied, and questions on periods of history not yet covered. I interrupted him when he did this, and when he asked other questions I thought were unfair. We became almost like two lawyers in a courtroom. Whenever I thought a question was out of line, I simply interrupted him. He glared at me, said nothing, and went on with his interrogation. Finally he came to some questions relevant to our studies and the students did very well. I think they were attempting to defend me and prove I had been a good teacher. I shall always remember how readily their hands went up.

The hour ended and, as we left the classroom for my office, I wondered if he might not reprimand me for the way I interrupted him. He merely looked at me sternly and, raising his voice, asked, "What are you planning to do in the future, Brother Tanner?" I replied that I wasn't exactly sure what my future profession would be. He then raised his voice again, "You would make a good lawyer!" Having said this, he turned abruptly and walked out of the building to his car. When I told this experience to a friend of mine that evening, he said, "I think he meant that you were not a very good seminary teacher and perhaps you had better study law." I was never sure whether or not my friend was right. This incident gives some idea of my disposition to be forthright and candid. I had had many experiences, in the past, of standing up for myself. Such a tendency can have results both good and bad. I'm not sure how I finally balanced out. In any case, I learned to fend for myself and take my chances.

Writing Seminary Textbooks

After teaching one year in Spanish Fork (1927–28), I enrolled in the University of Utah. To help pay my way at the university, I taught a half-day at the Granite High School LDS seminary. On one occasion, the commissioner of education, Joseph F. Merrill, came into my classroom. It was a large class of ninth-grade students. Our subject that day was the Old Testament story of David and Goliath. I was practical in my teaching. In this session I spent most of the hour on what might be called "Goliaths we face in our lives." I never believed much in miracles, so I used the story of David and Goliath to illustrate that all of us have occasional Goliaths to overcome. We must try to slay whatever Goliath makes our lives less than they could be, such as a bad temper, lying, or taking advantage of somebody. None of the class hour was spent on the question of whether there was a young man who used a sling to throw a rock that incapacitated a much larger man. I thought that may, or may not be true. Instead we spent our time on problems young people face here and now. I wanted to inspire the students to make good decisions.

The class helped me compile a list on the board of what they thought were their main Goliaths. As I remember, it was quite a list. When the class was over, Joseph F. Merrill, who had been sitting quietly in the back, came up and asked if I could write as well as my father. I quickly replied in the negative. He didn't accept my answer, because I later received a request to visit him in his office. He then asked me to write some textbooks for the junior high-school seminary students.

When I taught in the church seminary system, the students received academic credits toward their graduation from high school for these courses in religion. As a condition for students receiving academic credits, the church agreed that it would teach ethics and the broad field of biblical literature and avoid all denominational doctrines. As I talked with Commissioner Merrill in his office, I quickly discerned that one of his major interests was character education, the practical matter of teaching boys and girls to become responsible adults. He mentioned wanting a textbook that fostered discussion among the students. I understood his approach and prepared an outline of the book I intended to write. He seemed very pleased, accepted my plan, and I soon began writing.

Personally, I believe one cannot teach moral conduct as one can teach other subjects—simply by delivering knowledge. Rather, life situations must be presented and discussed, so the ideas become a part of the students' thinking and living. Commissioner Merrill gave me an office near his to write in, and I was completely happy searching for good quotations, poems, and literary models. I also enjoyed thinking about life situations, and thorny moral problems without easy solutions. I recall going into Commissioner Merrill's office and reading to him several such life situations. He smiled as I read them, and in a warm and friendly way said I was on the right track. The book was published in 1931 as *Problems of Youth*.

He asked me to write a second book almost immediately. I discussed this assignment with Adam S. Bennion and I recall that in the course of our conversation, Dr. Bennion said concerning the method I planned to use, "And they, the students, can look in on greatness as it is found in literature." It was from his remark that I took the title for my new book: *Looking in on Greatness*. Like the first, it contains case studies of moral problems young people face in their lives. In this book I started each chapter with two very controversial life situations, crucial and difficult for young people. I would add a brief clarification of the problem, then quote authors whose writings were relevant to its definition or solution.

I thought this was an effective way to teach moral conduct. I did not think one could effectively lecture young people on what they should do and not do. I thought it was better to present a situation, which they might later experience, allow them to think and reflect, and then present to them the consequences which might follow if they chose one course, and what the results might be if they made a different decision. I felt sure that just as the case method had been found to be the best method in teaching law, the Socratic method—where students are led, but not forced, toward conclusions—would be best in teaching character education. It might be called teaching by identification. The student identifies himself or herself with the situation, the particular problem, and then searches for a good solution. I stressed thinking about the consequences of actions.

It was my intent, though I never carried it out, to combine these two textbooks into a single volume on character education. Some day I hope this will happen. *Looking in on Greatness* was published in 1932 and reprinted several times. Both this book and *Problems of Youth* were used for many years in the junior seminary classes of the Mormon church.

My next undertaking was, for me, a much larger effort. This was to write a textbook on the New Testament, to be used by senior high-school students. I spent a little over a year in writing this book. It had 105 chapters. My father had written a two-volume work entitled *Old Testament Studies,* so I chose the title *New Testament Studies.*

I cannot overstate the importance of this assignment to me. I had some very deep convictions about Christ. By the time I was asked to write this book on the New Testament, I was in law school. I gladly withdrew from my legal studies. I felt writing such a book was more important than anything else I might do. I wanted to put the emphasis where I believed it would have the most meaning for young people. For me, this was a great opportunity. My overriding motivation was to give students an interpretation of Jesus that would make him their ideal, someone to whom they could give loyalty and whose life and teachings would enable them to understand the mission of the church itself.

I began with considerable preparation. I bought a good number of books and attempted to read everything I could find on each verse of the New Testament. I also had help from Margaret Gardner, the aunt of David P. Gardner, former president of the University of Utah and of the University of California. Margaret Gardner was teaching seminary in Delta, Utah. She came to Salt Lake to help me compile the material. Each day, for the first three hours, I would read all the material on a given verse or chapter in the New Testament, and then decide what material I wanted to quote or what emphasis I wanted to make. My approach was practical. I wanted the New Testament to relate to the current life of young people.

I believed that Jesus was, as one writer expressed it, "our eternal contemporary." The book was written during my first year of marriage, and I recall Grace would come to pick me up quite late in the evenings. I worked ten or twelve hours a day. I wanted to do an excellent job and I was consumed with joy and satisfaction over what I was doing. In my acknowledgements, I mentioned others who helped me—Burns Finlinson and Ed Barrett.

Joseph F. Merrill gave me great encouragement. I came to revere, respect, and love him for his confidence in me. He was not an easy man to become acquainted with. His formality and reserve were difficult to break through. But occasionally I caught a smile on his face and then I knew he approved of what I was trying to do.

Prior to becoming commissioner of education for the LDS church, Joseph F. Merrill had been dean of engineering at the University of Utah. Sometime after our acquaintance began, he was appointed, in 1931, to the position of apostle. He was a no-nonsense, orthodox Mormon, with a high regard for learning. He had no doubt that universities and Mormonism could do well together. While he was commissioner of education he brought to the Brigham Young University summer sessions the best teachers in religious studies from the Divinity School of the University of Chicago—Goodspeed in the New Testament, Graham in the Old Testament, and McNeil in church history. These fine scholars were involved primarily in teaching the seminary teachers. It was a bright period of fine scholarship for BYU, and for all the church.

The infusion of thought and scholarship from luminaries in the field of religion who were not Mormon was a bold venture. At the conclusion of three summers, one of the church leaders objected: "In teaching the gospel we can go and teach others at the University of Chicago, or they can come here to learn from us."

A Moral Dilemma

At this time I was given one of the highest tributes I ever received. Dr. Merrill asked me to go to the University of Chicago, get my Ph.D., and return as head of religious studies at BYU. I expressed my concern: "I would go to Chicago and in three years be forgotten." But Dr. Merrill was determined. A few days later he called me to his office and presented me with a letter signed by all three members of the First Presidency of the church, giving me financial assistance and a firm offer to teach as head of the Department of Religion at BYU. I asked for a few days to think it over. I am sure Commissioner Merrill expected me to be very pleased and accept the offer at once. I could see he was disappointed with my indecision. It was indeed an unusual letter and he was clearly pleased to have it signed by the top leaders.

The next few days I did a lot of soul searching. Could I spend the rest of my life reconciling Mormonism with the best scholarship? At that time I was studying law. I had conversations with Adam S. Bennion, my mentor and very dear friend. As usual, he did not try to give an answer, but simply suggested we "walk around the problem."

In my consideration of Dr. Merrill's generous offer, I was confronted with what seemed to be my perpetual dilemma, namely, how does one resolve a conflict between love of church and love of scholarship? In this case, while I loved my church, its members, and leaders deeply, my respect for academic learning had also deepened. My problem wasn't easy. I felt that a decision to accept his offer might someday compromise my intellectual integrity. This is not a unique problem for Mormonism. It is the eternal problem that affects countless persons who are committed to organized religion. My decision to turn down the Chicago-BYU offer carried with it a profound sadness.

A Great Friendship

One of the apostles of the LDS church at that time, David O. McKay, was reading my New Testament lessons. I did not know he was involved until one day, when I was in the elevator of the church office building, I saw some of the manuscript in his hand. I hesitated to speak to him, having never met him formally, but I nodded a greeting. He smiled and said, "I like these lessons you are writing." I replied that I was pleased and thanked him, and he said, "I hope some day you will come and see me." I replied that I would love to. Then he asked me why I had not done so before, and I replied that I was hesitant to take up any of his time. He smiled and again invited me to visit him. This was the beginning of a friendship that lasted to the end. It has been a cherished memory for me, a friendship of which I am very proud.

He once paid me a high compliment. It was early on a Sunday morning in 1935. I received a telephone call from him, and he said he would like to see me. I quickly volunteered to meet him wherever it would be most convenient for him. "No," he said, "I will call by at your home." We were living in a modest place. Soon he was at the front door. I was quite overwhelmed by such a distinguished visitor. After friendly greetings he said: "I want you to come to the church offices and write for the church. We will give you an office and secretary." I asked what I should write, and how long this assignment would take. Again, I was overwhelmed. "Just come down and write whatever may be needed," he replied. "For how long?" I asked. "Permanently," he answered. "All my life?" I asked. "Yes," he said with a warm smile.

I can't begin to describe my emotions. I loved and admired President McKay as no other man I had ever met. But all my life? I was then in my third year of law school. But there was a vastly greater problem. I knew in my heart that I did not possess sufficient faith to accept such an enormous assignment. How could I tell him? I loved my church. I wanted to please him. I had confidence I could do well in writing for the church. But I knew that I simply did not have enough orthodox conviction for such a lifetime assignment. Already my liberalism had caused trouble in the University Ward Sunday school class I was then teaching. My reply to President McKay was, "Suppose I were your son in his third year of law school, what would you advise him to do?" He discerned that my answer was negative, and we parted in the best of fellowship.

A Difficult Request

Several years after its publication, I was asked, in a letter, to revise my book, *New Testament Studies.* Specifically, I was instructed to "color it with Mormonism." I had written the text as a nondenominational study of the New Testament, so students could receive school credit for taking seminary courses in the public schools in Utah, Idaho, Arizona, and possibly elsewhere. No credit was given, nor was any asked, for the course on Mormon church history and doctrine. That study was denominational. My textbook had been written with the clear understanding that no reference to the Mormon church, or to any other church, would be made in such a way as to indoctrinate or proselyte. Having been asked originally, by Joseph F. Merrill, to produce a book that was nondenominational, I was surprised with this request.

I recall once seeing Dr. Merrill leaving the church office building with my text under his arm. He told me he was going to Boise to meet with the Idaho State Board of Education, to show them my book as proof that we taught a nondenominational course on the New Testament. I might add that I was very much in harmony with this goal. The universalism of Christ's teachings had always appealed to me. I believed this approach helped in character education and made good members of the church, which has always been the goal of studying the New Testament in LDS seminaries.

I answered the request by saying that I could not revise my text and "color it with Mormonism." Such an effort could not be made in good faith. I thought my forthright refusal would be the end of my writing textbooks. Instead I received a magnanimous, inclusive letter. It requested that I revise as I thought best. I felt very touched and moved by such a generous reply so I agreed to complete the revision. I hope I made improvements. Under a new title, *The New Testament Speaks,* it was published in 1935 and used by the LDS seminaries for twenty-nine years. I was very pleased that my book found such lasting approval. Later I was given the copyright of the book by David O. McKay, then president of the church.

Another revision of *The New Testament Speaks* was undertaken by my two colleagues, Sterling M. McMurrin and Lewis M. (Max) Rogers. In the preface, Dr. McMurrin wrote:

> . . . after numerous reprintings, Tanner considered publishing another revised, updated version. He invited his colleagues Rogers and McMurrin to join him in this venture. But rather than a conventional revision of *The New Testament Speaks,* we have produced a volume which is directed to a much larger audience and which introduces the reader to many of the problems that still trouble students of the New Testament.

This new volume, titled *Toward Understanding the New Testament,* published in 1990, is more historical than *The New Testament Speaks,* as it takes into account the great outpouring of scholarship on the New Testament over the past fifty-five years.

Christ's Ideals for Living

In 1955, I was asked once again to do some writing for the church. I recall the details of this assignment. I was in my business office on West Second South when the telephone rang. It was George R. Hill, general superintendent of the LDS Sunday schools, who asked if I would come and see him. I went immediately to his office and met with him and his two assistants, Lawrence McKay and Lynn Richards. After a few amenities George Hill asked me if I would be willing to write a manual for the Sunday schools. I was a little surprised; in fact, I was speechless. My business and my teaching at the university completely absorbed my time. For years, my thinking had been along the lines of the usual academic courses in philosophy. Such courses were quite independent of religious studies.

Why was I being asked now to write in the field of religion? I wondered if they had made a mistake in asking me, and suggested this as a possibility; perhaps they had another person in mind. I was sincere in raising these questions with them because it did not seem likely that people in such a high position would want me to write such an important manual. They explained that they were talking to the right person. I replied that I did not think I would be able to spare the time. Back of my thinking, of course, was the feeling I had that I may not write in a sufficiently orthodox way to be acceptable. For the preceding several years, as a teacher of courses in philosophy, neither my association nor my thinking had been in line with a particular religious position.

They explained that they were sure I would do a fine job. It was to be a manual or an outline or a textbook for college-age people on the teachings of Christ. To be sure this was a field in which I had a great interest. But I felt very reluctant to attempt such a task. For so many years, I had been a student and teacher at Stanford and the University of Utah. It had been about twenty years since I had taught and written

texts for the LDS church education department. After my negative reply, I had my hand on the door knob and I was about
to leave, aware that when I opened the door, I would have
turned down an opportunity, which I might later wish I had
accepted. At that moment, Superintendent Hill asked his associates: "Should we tell him?" They replied affirmatively. He
said, "We have been to President McKay and asked him to give
us the name of someone who could write the best text for our
college-age Sunday school classes on the subject of Christ's
teachings. Without hesitation he mentioned you as the one
who could do this."

I must say this surprised me. I loved President McKay. I
had seen him in many circumstances and I thought he always
came through with intelligence, perception, and compassion.
He had spoken at my Steven's funeral in 1949. I was not about
to turn him down on anything he might ask me to do. I went
back to where I had been sitting in front of them, and replied
that if President McKay asked me to do this, then I certainly
would comply with his request. I realized I was making a considerable commitment. I was accepting an assignment of work
that would be much different from teaching the usual courses
in a university philosophy department.

Many thoughts went through my mind as I left their
office. I was quite aware that it might be impossible for me
to write a manual or textbook for the Sunday schools that would
pass the church's reading committee. I had no objection to
such a committee—no objection to their holding careful
standards of orthodoxy and censoring anything that might
be questionable. That was their freedom. I was simply aware
that in recent years, friends of mine had attempted to write for
the church Sunday schools and seminaries and found that their
manuscripts were not approved. They had wasted their time
and labor.

For the next few days I thought a great deal about what
had been asked of me. I asked my friends and colleagues at the
university what they thought I should do. They replied that

they thought I should write the manual. But that didn't settle my mind. In religion, as in politics, and perhaps in all walks of life, people are divided between the liberals and conservatives. I was a liberal. The reading committee would probably be full of conservatives.

Within a week or so after meeting with Superintendent Hill, I had an opportunity to speak with President McKay. I asked if I might see him, and he replied, "Any time." The following morning we met in his office at eight o'clock. After a few pleasantries, he asked me what I wanted to see him about. I told him that I had been asked by the general superintendency of the Sunday schools to write a manual, but as I thought about it, I was quite convinced it would be difficult for me to write a manual that would please the reading committee. I said, "I feel very sure about this and I believe you understand that my concern has a real basis." He smiled, and then said something I shall always remember: "Well then, we will change the committee."

I was pleased with the great confidence and trust he expressed in me. Then I mentioned to him that I would need to have a good library in the field of the New Testament. I had previously made up my mind that if I were to accept this assignment I would like to have all the books that I could obtain, all that might help me in writing the manual. I told him I would need several thousand dollars to buy these books. Without hesitation he said, "Very well, whatever you need will be given to you. I shall arrange for you to buy whatever you think is desirable."

With such unlimited support, I left his office feeling that this was truly a remarkable assignment. I never in my life felt so determined to do a good job. For a year I think I almost overprepared. I went to bookstores all over the country—Yale, Princeton, Columbia, Chicago—and to used bookstores, wherever New Testament books were commonly sold. I ordered hundreds of books and charged them to the church. No one hesitated to give me whatever credit I needed.

I was given an office, a desk, and a secretary of long experience, Mrs. Marie Richards. After a few days we seemed to hit it off very well. When I was established in my new office, the books began to arrive.

One day the office secretary to Superintendent Hill, who was not aware of my appointment, at least not aware of the high source of my appointment, walked in my office waving a batch of invoices complaining that he was receiving more and more books for which he had no money to pay. He said, "This will simply have to stop. We haven't money in the budget to cover the cost of all these books." I explained that he should talk with Superintendent Hill. He returned shortly and assured me he would see that all the books I had ordered were paid for as promptly as they were received. The books constituted a beautiful addition to the Sunday school library on the New Testament.

After a few weeks, Mrs. Richards seemed rather nervous. She said in a reluctant way, "I think I should tell you that there is opposition to your writing this manual, and I am afraid you are spending all this labor, or will be spending it, in vain." I listened carefully, but knowing the authority of my appointment, I was not worried and asked her not to be bothered by such rumors. But she persisted and said, "There is a committee that has been organized to see that you do not write this manual, and some of the members of the committee are very high in church positions." I was still not disturbed and told her that I was sure everything would be all right. And everything did turn out well.

I spent many months reflecting on how I could structure a book that would be challenging and practical for teachers to use. When I finally thought of a title, *Christ's Ideals for Living,* it seemed to explain what I was trying to write. I divided each chapter into five parts: An introduction to the ideal itself as found in world literature, the ideal as expressed in New Testament scriptures, the ideal as lived in Christ's life, the ideal if lived in our lives, and finally, the ideal in quotations from church leaders. I collected an enormous amount of material to help me in each part of each chapter.

The day arrived for the final manuscript to be approved by the reading committee. It turned out that President McKay had indeed appointed a new group, with Adam S. Bennion as chairman. He and I spent part of several days reviewing the suggestions made by the committee.

As we turned over each page there were, of course, a number of suggestions, marked with a blue pencil—sometimes just a question mark, sometimes a stricture, and sometimes a matter of correction. When we came across each one of these blue marks, we would discuss whatever had been checked. Sometimes it was an error on my part, such as the proper meaning for the church of the words *eternal life,* as distinguished from the meaning of the word *immortality.* I was very pleased to be corrected in matters about which I was not as well versed or as well informed as perhaps I should have been. I was also pleased with any suggestion that made for greater clarity.

But once in a while there would be a stricture concerning something I had written which I felt very deeply about. This was the interesting and vital part of our mutual examination of the manuscript. Our procedure was that whenever we came to a mark made by the reading committee, Adam Bennion would read aloud what I had written. Occasionally it would be something I felt was important to Christianity. I had some strong beliefs about the teachings of Christ. I had written in this field earlier and had come to know the subject quite well. I had taught New Testament literature at Stanford. I had deep convictions about the meaning of religion itself, and about the Christian religion in particular. So when there were blue pencil marks that disputed my interpretations, I naturally looked at them very carefully. Sometimes a change or suggestion would be a matter of great importance to me. I did not intend to have my manuscript altered in ways with which I did not agree. The issue was one of personal integrity

When I had such reservations, Adam Bennion and I would consider the matter, and when he saw I was emotionally involved and felt deeply about it, he would make a mark with the letter *s*. I soon learned that the letter *s* meant the author would "stand," not change his statement. Sometimes I felt that my convictions, both as a scholar and as a religious person, were at stake. It was then the procedure for Adam S. Bennion to present those parts marked with an *s* to President McKay for his final decision. I recall that President McKay agreed with all my interpretations.

Once when we were going over the manuscript, Adam Bennion said, "You know that I am chairman of this reading committee for only one purpose." This pleased me very much. I was glad he felt it worth his time and that the book itself would be of value to the church. With my efforts in writing this book, I came to believe that the basic Christian ideals were compatible with the LDS religion. No doubt many ideals are not fully realized, but that is the way it is with a great ideal. It is beyond our reach. We simply aspire to its achievement. Mormonism refers to such an upward reach as the law of eternal progression. An example would be the great ideal of equality. Our understanding and practice of this principle has, in recent years, been greatly improved. This improvement illustrates eternal progression.

A footnote to the story is that in the year following publication, I decided I could afford to pay for all the books I had purchased for the church, and so I sent a check sufficient to cover their costs. In the letter thanking me for the gift, Superintendent George R. Hill stated: "I regard this book *[Christ's Ideals for Living]* as the finest manual yet produced as a Sunday school text. I predict that it will be regarded as one of the most valuable texts for Sunday schools and general church use, for years to come . . . It was a genuine pleasure to be associated in a small way with you in this most scholarly production."

The manual expresses beliefs fundamental to Christianity and the Mormon religion. It attempts the impossible task of trying to explain the various ways in which Christ himself would help us solve our daily problems. It is one more venture with the New Testament, another effort to write about the Christian ethic. In essence, it is a textbook concerned with practical religion. I wanted the reader—whether student or teacher—to participate in the ideal, that is, to discover some new insight and make his or her own interpretation. My hope is expressed in this aphorism: The better the book the more room for the reader.

My hidden ambition was to write more on philosophy. That was a dream that never came true. I was giving too much of my time at the university and building the O. C. Tanner Company. In *One Man's Search*, I wrote a little on truth claims and value judgments—the work of every good student in philosophy—but more than this was not possible.

In any case, perhaps the most useful book I leave is *Christ's Ideals for Living*.

Chapter Six

To Stanford, in Search of Better Answers

. . .

Chapter Six

To Stanford, in Search of Better Answers

The unexamined life is not worth living.

—Plato

■ ■ ■

A New Journey

In January, 1936, the day I was sworn in as a member of the Utah Bar, I came home with a rather surprising announcement:

"Grace, I want to pack up and leave here for a great university."

"Where?" she asked rather stunned.

"I don't know—maybe Berkeley," I replied.

"Why do you want to do that?" she asked.

I replied, "I feel so ignorant. I know so little. I want to be better informed. I want to be able to judge ideas critically. I need to know more about how to respond to persuasive arguments. In the world of ideas, I feel so poorly informed. I need a better education."

"How can we ever do this—just pick up and go? We can't afford it. I just can't leave," she said in dismay. "I'm going to have another baby and I must have some security!"

That stopped me momentarily. We have smiled many times about her response, and agree that it was almost the only time I was seriously questioned on practical matters. She probably always had too much confidence in me, and this was the first time she came right out and expressed any doubt. We were happy to be expecting another baby. We both wanted a nice family.

But I had given a great deal of thought to going away for further study. The problem was not our limited resources, but how I felt about myself. Deep inside me was a yearning for a better understanding of the world—its religions, politics, economics, and philosophies. I felt my ignorance in these subjects so acutely; it was almost painful. I think no one could have loved universities more than I. When I was a missionary in Germany, I passed by a great university every morning on my way to meetings. It was located behind high brick walls. Occasionally I would try to look through the gates or over the walls, with an overwhelming curiosity about what they were reading and teaching. If only I could know! I promised myself that some day I would find out.

So I determined to leave Utah, go to California, and there search for what I thought was better than gold—ideas, theories, values, truths. I wanted to study in a great university.

At the time, it seemed to me that law was primarily a study of precedents. In legal studies we seldom asked, nor were we told, why a law was good or bad. This was what I wanted to know. Even my study of religion had begun and ended with presuppositions, of which I was not certain. I wanted to know what the best scholars had to say about these various religious assumptions. I wanted to know more of history. I wanted a good foundation for my beliefs, the best I could find.

Grace understood, although she did point out that a law degree should be quite enough to satisfy anyone. But I was far from satisfied! I simply could not see my way into a satisfying future, unless I found answers to some of the major questions that had plagued me for years. Many times, Grace has remarked to others that a good husband is one who enjoys what he is doing. She reconciled with my decision and we have never looked back. A new world of adventure opened up for ten years. I studied at Stanford and Harvard, and enjoyed several years of teaching at Stanford as well.

Prior to leaving Utah, I had done well in building the O. C. Tanner Company. I had repeat customers at various high schools. My employees were quite dependable. Above all, Grace and I decided we could go on with a normal family life. While the future was not certain, it looked quite favorable. Two of our children were born in Palo Alto, and one while we attended Harvard.

The Great Depression

The Great Depression dominated the opinions and judgments of people at that time. There were "brain trusts" in government, and businessmen seemed to be at a loss for solutions to the country's economic problems. During this period a vast range of political and economic ideas was being explored. Communism was examined along with socialism and capitalism, all with their many variations. These systems were widely considered as possible options, different ways of organizing society, alternatives that might alleviate human suffering and economic stagnation. At this time, the Soviet variety of communism had not yet been fully understood outside the USSR. Real awareness of the tension between individual liberty and authoritarian central planning came much later, although suspicions about conditions under communist rule were beginning to surface. The thirties were a time of open season on all ideas. As I write about this period of history, I wonder if the nineties may be another era of social crisis, a time when people are again searching for better answers.

The year 1936 was also a time of personal adventure for me. I was determined to explore new ideas. To do this, I selected the broad discipline of philosophy. Like Descartes, the founder of modern philosophy, my method was to wipe the slate clean of past ideas. I doubt now if this "clean slate" plan, of believing, with Descartes, only "clear and distinct ideas," is possible. But as I look back, it worked to a remarkable degree for me. I was willing to reexamine everything, and I was certain a university would be the best place to search for better answers.

On the morning of February 4, Grace and I, with our two-year old son, Dean, left Salt Lake City in our Ford, bound for Berkeley, California. A great amount of snow had fallen the night before, and it was still snowing. The roads were barely passable. Near Wells, Nevada, we hit a snowdrift and ran off the road, but we made it safely to Elko. Early the next morning it was eight degrees below zero. It was dark by the time we found a motel in Sacramento.

I recall the misgivings I felt that evening. Generally I was not lacking in self-confidence, but in that Sacramento motel room I really wondered if I were making a big mistake. As I played on the bed with Dean, who was his usual cheerful self, I felt I might be whistling in the dark. I didn't buckle, but I bent a little. I never did let Grace know how shaken I was. Ahead was a world completely unknown to me.

The next morning we arrived in Berkeley and stopped near the campus of the University of California. Classes were changing and the campus was crowded. As I walked by the offices of the philosophy department I could not find anyone with whom to talk. The halls were crowded, jammed with students. I returned to the car.

Stanford and Harvard, 1936–45

When Grace and I were on our honeymoon in 1931, we had stopped at Stanford University in Palo Alto. It was early evening and we sat in Memorial Church and listened to an organ recital. As we left, I recall pausing outside to look more carefully at the church. I was standing near enough to touch one of the large stones of which it was built. I recall thinking to myself that the sermons preached here to a university audience must be very intelligent. I would like to hear one of them. This must be a church quite acceptable to everyone. I stood there only a moment, and in my heart I had a wish, barely a flicker, that I might some day return to Stanford. It was a fleeting thought, quite beyond serious consideration, but it never left me. I did not imagine that some day I would be a chaplain and preach sermons in that beautiful chapel.

In Berkeley, when I returned to the car where Grace was waiting, I announced: "We're going to drive over to Stanford before I register here." At Stanford, Grace again waited in the car. I parked on a side road near the philosophy department. It was a quiet afternoon. I met an impressive-looking professor, Henry Waldgrave Stuart, head of the department. We spent an hour in unhurried conversation, and I made up my mind. "We're staying here," I announced when I returned to the car. We found a modest house in Barron Park, and thus our years at Stanford began.

One of my teachers, Harold Chapman Brown, was a Marxist. Another, Henry Waldgrave Stuart, had misgivings about the conclusions of Karl Marx. With such a difference between two highly respected scholars, I soon saw I had not lost ambiguity in the clear light of reason. Between classes, on the inner quad of Stanford, just outside the doors of the philosophy department, I stood with classmates and argued with seemingly endless energy—somewhat as I did when studying law. But now the stakes were higher, at least for me. We were not discussing a law case in order to become good lawyers; we were examining ideas for their truth, and social systems for their justice. To be sure, from lectures and my reading, I hoped I might build a sound philosophy of my own. Sometimes I walked with a professor to his car, or across the quad, seeking some additional refinement of an idea expressed in his lecture. I loved those opportunities.

As an escape from the sedentary life in the library, I played handball and tennis. That beautiful campus, its library, my teachers and fellow students—all this I regarded as sheer paradise. When I left Stanford after nine years as a student and teacher, I was convinced that no one had ever been given so much.

I worked hard and I obtained at least one profound insight. It happened while I was studying with a visiting professor, the distinguished American legal philosopher, Morris Cohen, from the City College of New York. His classes were a riot of clashing ideas. No matter what idea was expounded or defended, he would shoot it down. Sometimes I thought I could argue that he had been inconsistent. But he would overwhelm me with his erudition and his belief in the principle of polarity. Finally, I got his message. There are no unassailable propositions. All systematic philosophies are vulnerable. I realized that I had been traveling on the wrong road. I came to see that technically and logically, there were no final answers. At best there were probabilities, and though some are high probabilities, yet in strict logic, the best answers we can find are never certainties.

I learned much more from Morris Cohen. As a teacher, he was a genius. Ideas flew back and forth in his class in the best Socratic tradition. I loved it, even when I was wounded in the crossfire. After my experience in Cohen's class, I gave up my search for final answers. In my judgment, Cohen was America's ranking scholar on jurisprudence. I read his famous book on that subject and did my master's thesis under him ("An Ethical Basis for the Rule of Liability Without Fault"). In it I challenged the well-established legal principle that liability depends upon culpability, that, for example, there must be blameworthiness before someone can be required to pay for an injury. Such blameworthiness may be no more than a rather remote negligence, but there must be, according to common law, a proximate cause to connect the wrongdoer to the damage. The contention of my thesis was that this principle may be challenged. In many modern life situations, injuries can be caused without real wrongdoing. One of my arguments was that whenever an individual or entity changes or upsets the quiet and peaceful order of things, as a contractor does when he begins construction, that individual or entity should be held liable for any injury suffered as a result of the changes he initiates. This was the gist of my treatise. Such an idea has now become an accepted part of modern litigation, as illustrated in a manufacturer's liability.

Morris Cohen accepted my thesis with the comment "a very scholarly work." I was pleased. I assumed my thesis would eventually become a chapter of a longer dissertation for my Ph.D. But when I was asked to teach at Stanford, I gave myself entirely to that work. I was overwhelmed with this opportunity. Later I was in such a hurry to return to my business in Salt Lake, that I took a chance and did not compile my bibliography. My friend, Sam Thurman, then a teacher at the Stanford Law School and later dean of the University of Utah College of Law, once said, "Obert, you must have taken out every book on jurisprudence from our Stanford Law Library. I noted your signature on almost every card."

My experience with Cohen had a profound effect on my life. I became aware there are no final or simple answers. In a way this was a big relief to me. I needed his scrubbing of my earlier-held ideas. I might add that I later tried to follow Cohen's method of teaching. His was a combination of the case method used in the study of law, and the Socratic method as used in teaching philosophy.

At one point during my time in Palo Alto, I ran out of money, and when a letter came from Salt Lake with the bad news that a promised loan would not be forthcoming, I said to Grace, "We'd better pack up. We've just enough travel money to get us back to Utah." Our second child, Joan, had been born a few weeks before. We packed the car, and as we were leaving, I thought of a book I wanted to buy, so we stopped at the old Stanford bookstore. As I pushed my way through one of its swinging doors, my book in hand, I saw one of Stanford's great teachers, R. D. Harriman. I barely heard him say, as he pushed through the other half of the swinging door, "Congratulations, Tanner." I turned and followed him to where he had paused, in front of some shelves of books. I asked him what he had said when we passed. He answered: "I said congratulations, you were just awarded a scholarship."

With this good news, I rushed to the car where Grace was waiting with our two children. "We're staying," I announced in triumph. "I've been granted a scholarship."

In 1937 I had an opportunity to study philosophy at Harvard. One of my teachers there was Clarence Irving Lewis. He invited Grace and me to his home for Thanksgiving, and it was the beginning of a lasting friendship, both with him and with his wife, Mabel. Later we enjoyed their visits to Salt Lake and together we shared vacations in southern Utah. Professor Lewis thought this part of the country the most beautiful place on earth. He was a near-professional photographer and for years his photographs hung on the walls of the motel office in Fruita near Capitol Reef National Park.

I have always been something of a hero worshiper, and certainly one of my heroes was C. I. Lewis. His books rank among the best, if not the best, to come from Harvard's philosophy department. Lewis was a philosopher's philosopher. In gratitude for what he taught me, and because of his reputation as a teacher, I later requested that the Tanner Lectures on Human Values at Harvard be dedicated to his memory. Each year Harvard sends me the program of the Tanner Lectures. I am proud of the dedication that appears on the cover of the lecture program. After he retired from Harvard, Professor Lewis taught part-time at Stanford. He left his books to the Tanner Library of Philosophy. His portrait is on the wall of that library. Later Grace and I were honored to establish the Mabel Lewis Periodical Library in Emerson Hall at Harvard.

When I returned from my year of studying philosophy at Harvard, I received an offer to teach at Stanford, in the Department of Religious Studies. I was delighted. Until then I had been interested in learning for my own improvement, now I wanted to share what I had learned with others. I felt so honored to be a teacher where I had once been a student. Working out a new course was a challenge and a real joy. I did not keep a complete list of the courses I taught there, but they included philosophy of religion, comparative world religions, history of religions, New Testament literature, and contemporary problems in religion.

My special ambition was to make my class on comparative religions a popular one. I would take the students on buses to San Francisco, there to visit various places of worship— Shinto, Buddhist, Catholic, Protestant, Jewish, etc. Whoever was in charge of a specific church at the time of our visit would invite us to sit near the altar or pulpit and give the students adequate time to ask questions. I recall telling them that they could never really learn about religion until they interviewed those whose lives were dedicated to their faiths. We had interesting experiences talking with the leaders of various religious groups. The students did all the questioning. They seemed to enjoy it. In this class, the students also wrote their textbook. Each student selected a particular subject, such as the idea of good, of evil, of God, or of immortality—any doctrine considered fundamental to a particular religion. I provided specific library references on their chosen subject, and they were expected to become a good scholar on that particular subject. I compiled the best papers as a textbook, which required a part-time secretary. Thus each class produced its own volume, and they often asked me to autograph it. I was understandably proud to see the class become large with interested students.

At last, I was asked by the chaplain to take his position while he was on leave. I had already decided to return to Utah, however, so I declined. Stanford's acting president, Al Eurich, later requested that I come back as acting chaplain and I did for a limited time. I recall that besides my work as chaplain, I volunteered to continue the classes I had formerly taught. It took all my energies to prepare a sermon each Sunday, and then teach classes during the week. I modeled my sermons after those of Harry Emerson Fosdick which followed the pattern of addressing an individual's problem. It was a kind of pastoral counseling adapted to the pulpit. I liked this form of preaching.

While I went to Stanford to gain a wider perspective, and while I did take the opportunity to examine again my own religious heritage, sometimes with painful results, I maintained links to my tradition. Evidence of this is the following letter dated January 31, 1945. It was written when I accepted the assignment of acting chaplain at Stanford University. The letter read:

> We hereby authorize you as an Elder in the Church of Jesus Christ of Latter-day Saints, now a Chaplain in the Memorial Church at the Stanford University, California, to perform the marriage ceremony in any case in which you as a minister of the Gospel may be authorized to perform a marriage ceremony by the laws of the United States or by the rules and regulations issued by proper authority thereunder.
>
> > Sincerely yours,
> > Heber J. Grant
> > J. Reuben Clark
> > David O. McKay
> > The First Presidency

It seemed a little sad to me, that among students taking courses in philosophy, there was an atmosphere of apology when we talked about religion. Religion did not have the standing of careful scholarship and logical analysis associated with courses in philosophy. I understand the differences between the disciplines. Religion is a way of living while philosophy is a way of thinking. Religion is a search for the good life, philosophy is a search for truth. In the minds of many, religion is associated with beliefs in magic and a whole world of unverifiable claims. Other students identify religion with the moral and ethical, the upward reach of people seeking the noblest in human life. If there is one discipline of mixed variety and quality, that surely is religion.

A Lasting Legacy

My years of study at Stanford and Harvard shaped much of my personal philosophy. I admit now that I over-estimated the value of graduate work in these universities, but this high expectation did give me strong motivations. I was looking for Truth, spelled with a capital *T,* and searching for the Good Society, one that would be without such failures as were experienced in the Great Depression. I was asking for too much, but it took years before I discovered this. Now I am quite certain that truth is spelled with a small *t,* that there are many truth possibilities, and also that there are various roads that lead to a good society. I have learned to live with questions and settle for probabilities, the best probabilities I can find. And I cherish my certainties, some of which have lived with me for many years. In the end I did not find many final answers in great universities, but I did learn to love the questions.

At Stanford I learned much about social responsibility. The failures in our democracy were made clearer to me as I studied the Great Depression. But when I came back from that decade of searching, I found I still had my commitment to the value of individualism. I became aware of the importance of a good balance between the personal and the social. Yet with all our social problems, I came to believe with Ayn Rand, "Civilization is the progress of a society towards privacy." I recall a statement by Justice Brandeis, "The right most prized by civilized man is the right to be left alone." I am glad I tried to keep this balance. Today I measure the highest quality of a civilization by its emphasis on individualism.

Several events had caused me to consider moving back to Utah. We lost our Dean to polio. From that loss, a lot of joy went out of our lives. My mother lived near us in Palo Alto and she passed away. World War II was ending. It was a time of social change when people sought new foundations for their lives. I began to wonder if I really wanted to spend the rest of my life at Stanford teaching the same courses over and over again, year after year. I love adventure. I take on a challenge rather easily. Back home I could give more attention to my company. I never lost my dream of a great company.

I knew I might regret leaving Stanford the rest of my life. Palo Alto is a beautiful city. We were acquainted with most of its streets, patronized its shops and the movie house, picnicked in the countryside where great oak trees flourished, and enjoyed seeing the long beautiful passenger trains as they traveled between San Francisco and Los Angeles. (I love trains.) In summertime I recall the soft breezes from the ocean a few miles away, the beautiful beaches for relaxation, Half Moon Bay, the vast Pacific Ocean, Golden Gate Bridge, Golden Gate Park, and Seal Rock. And Stanford itself, the teaching I loved so much.

I returned to Utah without completing work for my Ph.D. I have thought many times, that this was a mistake. However that may be, I chose an option that turned out better than I expected. I decided to build a strong Tanner Company. In the preceding eighteen years, I had made good progress with the company, but now, if I returned to Utah, I might eventually build a great company. I thought about being able to serve good causes. I could do this if my company were as successful as I thought it could be. I never stopped dreaming and hoping and wondering about the future. I decided to take my chances. It was a big ambition.

Happily, I did not have to give up teaching altogether. I had an invitation to teach at the University of Utah. My plan was to teach with the rank of lecturer. This would give me time with the company. A lecturer is paid only for the lecture given.

He has no obligation to remain on campus, or serve on faculty committees. At noon I would leave the campus and go downtown to do what was needed in solving my company's problems, of which there were many. One might say I just continued my dual life of teaching and business. I loved both; especially as the company improved my chances to help with causes I cared about. This improvement in my financial situation, and what I could do as a result, helped to set some new goals for my life. I tell about this in the last chapter of this book.

I did leave Stanford, but I have returned often, enjoying the satisfactions of having a child and a grandchild study there, and being able to support the beauty and to assist the work of that great university. I prize a few words spoken by Richard Lyman, president of Stanford at the dedication of a fountain I donated:

> ... I view today's ceremonies as both a celebration and a vindication of Obert Tanner's persistent view that a seat of learning deserves—indeed requires—beautiful places where the members of its community may pause to look, to rest, and to meditate.
>
> The Tanner Fountain provides just this kind of a place. . . . I predict . . . that it will henceforth be a principal campus landmark, fulfilling your dreams, Obert, and providing for generations to come a most fitting memorial to your son, Dean, and that touch of grace and beauty for which you have been a persistent advocate. . . .
>
> My own remarks would not be complete without adding my thanks not only for the fountain, but also for your other services to this University, as a member of its faculty, as acting chaplain, as the provider and sustainer of the Tanner Library

in the Philosophy Department, and as the donor
of the Tanner Lectureship. You are a staunch and
stalwart friend of Stanford. You are also a man of
conviction and principle, and Stanford is proud
to have benefitted from your wisdom and to have
merited the friendship and support you have so
generously provided over the years.

The University of Utah, 1945–74

In 1945, I began my longest period of teaching in one
place, twenty-nine years. Philosophy can create problems for
students with conservative traditions, be they political,reli-
gious,or economic. It is always considering new possibilities
and reconsidering the validity of old ones. This can be upset-
ting to people who already have deeply held beliefs. At Stanford the students were brilliant, as they were at the University
of Utah, but Utah students are more conservative, particularly in religion. I considered this a plus for a teacher who enjoys
lively discussions. An open mind, an attitude of the tentative
and provisional, is not the usual attitude of those with a strong
religious faith. Some students were warned not to take classes
in philosophy, especially the philosophy of religion. Parents
and friends fear the loosening of ties among those they care
deeply about.

My largest class was in the philosophy of religion. I tried
to teach it with the same objectivity one might find in a class
at Harvard, Chicago, or Stanford, and I think I enjoyed the
same freedom teachers have there. I do not recall a single
comment or innuendo that was intimidating to my freedom as
a teacher. There was plenty of dissent and argument among
students themselves, as there should be, but there was never
a hint of censorship from the university administration, nor
from the community. For that I was grateful. The least degree

of censorship would have been unbearable. I also gave seminars on individual philosophers—Plato, Kant and William James. My seminar on Kant was the challenge I enjoyed most. I had studied Kant with Lewis at Harvard.

I did not hesitate to discuss a religious belief, as such, if it were within a dialogue that belonged in the course. But I felt it would be out of bounds if I were to volunteer negative criticism beyond the borders of the subject being taught. This limitation seemed especially important in teaching the philosophy of religion. Even so, complete objectivity for any teacher is quite impossible. One can only try at it. My favorite compliment was the comment of a student, as he handed me his blue book, after the final examination: "I sure would like to know what you personally think about some of the subjects we talked about." I felt that on the great issues we examined the students must come to their own views, that it would be inappropriate for a teacher to go beyond discussion and discourse.

I was treated well by the university. In 1956 I was given a full professorship and in 1974 the rank of professor emeritus. I prize a letter written to me on April 9, 1974.

> In recognition of your many contributions to your department and the University, your faculty colleagues have recommended and the University's Institutional Council has approved your appointment, effective July 1, 1974, as a Professor Emeritus of Philosophy. Your formal retirement from the University faculty at the end of the 1973–74 academic year affords me a special opportunity to express appreciation for your service to this institution over a period of 29 years.
>
> On behalf of the Institutional Council, I wish also to recognize the great value of your generous support for the University of Utah, of your

public commitment to the quest for knowledge and wisdom, and of your devotion to beauty. May the coming years bring you increasing happiness in all of your worthy endeavors.

With kindest personal regards.

Sincerely yours,
David Pierpont Gardner
President

Some of Tanner's fountains: (clockwise) Harvard University; Hansen Planetarium; Marriot Library, University of Utah; LDS church office building.

Tanner Fountain at Memorial Hall, Stanford University.

Tanner Fountain at Abravanel (Symphony) Hall.

The Tanner Company's first home on Fenway Avenue.

Offices of the O. C. Tanner Company, Capitol Theatre building.

First Tanner Company building on South State Street.

Current world headquarters of the O. C. Tanner Company.

O. C. Tanner with Eleanor Roosevelt at a United Naions function.

*The Tanner family in 1988: (clockwise from top left) Joan, David,
Carolyn, Obert, Grace.*

Grace and Obert Tanner at home.

Chapter Seven

ENTREPRENEUR

. . .

Chapter Seven

ENTREPRENEUR

. . . We must take the current when it serves,

Or lose our ventures.

—William Shakespeare

∎ ∎ ∎

Introduction

I started in the jewelry business at the age of seventeen, obtaining a job as an errand boy and clerk in a jewelry store. When the store was busy with many customers, I was allowed to sell inexpensive jewelry items. That first job was seventy-two years ago. The year was 1921.

I started my own jewelry company six years later, in 1927. I sold high school seniors their graduation class rings and pins. Fifteen years later I shifted from school jewelry to corporate recognition awards purchased by companies to present to employees for their years of service and other achievements. This has been the specialty of my company for the past fifty years.

In sixty-six years, the company has grown from one employee to more than two thousand. This large number of people is one reason I was moved to write my autobiography. People beyond my family and a few close friends, may wonder how the company started, and what kept it going. I have wanted my company to benefit all those whose lives are affected by it—family, employees, customers, and the community beyond. What follows is a brief account of the history of the O. C. Tanner Company.

I began my company as an entrepreneur, and it has remained an entrepreneurship up to the present time. The dictionary defines an entrepreneur as, "One who organizes, manages, and assumes all the risks of a business or enterprise." This has been my role as founder and leader of the O. C. Tanner Company. I made the important decisions, saw them through, and assumed the risks.

By choice and by accident, I found myself within the large field of employer/employee relations. The use of recognition awards in corporate life was a new idea. We were pioneers in this field. *Pioneer* is a word I like personally because of my family heritage. It may describe my disposition and indicate something of the special way in which I was an entrepreneur.

In the beginning of the O. C. Tanner Company, I was a teacher doing a little moonlighting. I had no business school training, no capital, no customers, no blueprint to follow, not even a familiar product. On the other hand, I did have a valuable training experience—years working on a dairy farm, laying track on a railroad, doing carpentry, missionary work, teaching, and writing. All were jobs that later helped me survive as an entrepreneur.

A Chance Meeting

It is sometimes difficult to choose an event that marks the beginning of a company's history. I might go back to the day when I began my college education. It was an event I could describe as a chance meeting with a stranger.

In the fall of 1921, I registered at the University of Utah. Just in front of me, in a line of students marked "freshman" was a young man in a red sweater soiled with coal dust. His modest appearance gave me courage to share with him my overriding concern. "Have you found a job?" I asked.

"Yes," he replied. "I take care of furnaces in homes near the university."

"How much do you make?" I asked. "Oh, from three to four dollars per week for each home," he said. "I go in and stoke up the furnace in the evening, and early in the morning I shake up the fire so the house will be warm when the people get up." At that time coal was used for heating purposes.

"Would you mind if I tried to get a job like that, so long as I do not call on your customers?"

"That would be okay," he replied, "I'll give you the list of homes I work for." With the help of his generous offer, I found work near the university. I never met this young man again. I asked a question, a brief conversation followed, and I found employment, yet that event turned out to have a long series of consequences.

After a few months of tending furnaces, I became a little restless to find a better job, where I might earn and learn at the same time. I thought the well-to-do people whose furnaces I tended might give me a lead to something better.

The first person I approached was William Schubach, who owned one of the jewelry stores in the city. I asked his son, a boy about ten years old, to ask his father to come down to the furnace room. Mr. Schubach came to the basement in black tie and was clearly disturbed that I had interrupted his evening. I apologized and then put my case to him as briefly as possible. I told him I had had sales experience, house-to-house selling, and would like a job in his jewelry store. With all the self-assurance I could muster, I asserted: "I think I would do a good job for you as a salesman." To my surprise, Mr. Schubach gave me a job.

A Close Call

After the first few months my employer seemed to have a growing conviction that I was not as good a salesman as he had hoped I would be. I sensed his disappointment, and recall saying to my mother, "I have to make good, Mother, because if I fail, I'll never be a success at anything."

One Saturday, after the store was closed, the bad news came. My employer said, "Tanner, here is your pay. I won't be needing you any more." He handed me, or tried to hand me, my week's wages, the usual five-dollar bill, and two one-dollar bills. I didn't reach to take the money, and he said, "Here's your money. What's the matter, don't you want your pay?" I asked him why he was firing me, and he replied, "Oh, Tanner, you'll find something. You're not cut out to be a salesman."

"I think I can sell," I responded. Mr. Schubach replied, "No, Tanner, salesmen are born, they're not made. You're just not a salesman. Here's your money, don't you want it? I thought that evening in my basement, when you asked for a job, that I had found a salesman. I was mistaken."

I still didn't move to take the bills he waved at me. Inwardly I was resentful about his decision, and a flood of words began to pour forth. I recall very clearly what I said. One doesn't forget statements made when scolding one's boss. I stated my objections to being fired and made my case that I was being treated unfairly. "It's no wonder you are disappointed," I said, "the way you treat me. When I have a customer you interrupt me which makes it so nobody could sell. You come up beside me and listen to every word I say, and then you get closer, until I feel I must turn the customer over to you. I'm a better salesman than you are. I've watched you sell and I can do better."

For the first time he looked directly at me. (He had a habit of not looking at people when he spoke.) He turned to his main salesman, Lincoln White, who was fixing the Saturday window display at the front of the store and said, "My God, Lincoln, this kid has gone and sold me again! He sold me when I met him in my furnace room at home. Now he's gone and sold me again! He wants another chance! What shall I do?" I don't think Mr. Schubach was asking for advice so much as expressing his personal frustration. Mr. White gave me an assist: "I guess any man is entitled to a second chance."

"All right," my employer said, "here's your pay for the week. You come back next Monday." I took the money, happy and grateful for a reprieve. I was back on Monday, and my employer stayed away from me when I had a customer. My self-confidence had been restored. I was so pleased. With my new beginning, I thought I could sell anything, including items in the store that had remained unsold for a long time, stored away in drawers or on shelves. Whenever I suggested to a customer a low price on one of these items, it pleased my employer for a chance to get rid of it. Now, on Saturday evenings, when he gave me the seven dollars, I could tell he was pleased, but giving a compliment was not easy for Mr. Schubach. He was severe and demanding. With him I had a good apprenticeship.

Two years later I decided to give more attention to my studies at the university. Mr. Schubach offered me a share of the store's profits if I would remain, but I declined. A university education was the goal of my life. So in 1923 I left the jewelry business and did not return to it until 1927. I did other things for the next few years: served a mission for my church, sold savings bonds, worked as a carpenter, and other jobs.

Teaching and Moonlighting with Jewelry

In 1927, I was principal of the LDS seminary in Spanish Fork. My salary was eighteen hundred dollars for the year, fairly good pay at that time. I was in debt to the Davis County Bank for a loan of five hundred dollars. My mother had negotiated this loan by mortgaging her house so that I could take an extended trip to the Near East and several countries in Europe after my mission. I had wanted this trip, and my mother wanted me to have it. But now I faced the burden of paying back the loan. I could see that with my teaching salary, it would take much longer than a year to repay it so that I could return to my first ambition of attending the university.

I began to explore opportunities for additional work while teaching—in other words, moonlighting. I was boarding at the home of Mrs. Mattley in Spanish Fork. There were several other boarders at her home, including a dentist, a school supervisor, the manager of the sugar factory, and a cashier in the bank. One evening around our dinner table, there was unusual laughter and good cheer. I waited until the other boarders were gone to ask Mrs. Mattley why everyone was so cheerful.

"Don't you know?" she replied. "They invested their savings in a mine in Eureka and it struck a rich vein of gold and silver." This mine later became well known as the "Eureka Lily." I felt a little left out that evening, but I had no money to invest, only a debt for my European travels, and hardly any paid on that.

That evening as I walked up the street from Mrs. Mattley's home, a little despondent at my slow financial progress, a thought came to me, something like a flash of lightning. At the moment, I recall I was standing next to the post office. I thought, why not do a little moonlighting, selling class rings to nearby high schools? My earlier experience as a clerk in a jewelry store could help me.

Birth of the Company

That brainstorm, in the fall of 1927, was the beginning of the O. C. Tanner Company. I went to Salt Lake the next Saturday and asked a jewelry manufacturing shop, the Dennis Company, if they would make some high school class pins for me. They consented and gave me a few samples of gold block letters that were suitable for high school and seminary graduation pins. Springville Seminary gave me my first order for fifty pins. I charged them two dollars and twenty-five cents each, for a ten-karat gold *S* with a chain and numeral *28* attached as a guard. The pins cost me two dollars, so I made a profit of twenty-five cents on each. The profit on the whole order was twelve dollars and fifty cents.

I recall how thrilled I was with this first success in my new venture. Up to this time, I had frugally avoided spending the dollar eighty-five for a round-trip ticket between Spanish Fork and Salt Lake City. Weekends in a small town, for a single person, can be very lonely. Now I was in business! I had a new interest and the future looked bright. With my salary and the sale of seminary pins and class rings, I was able to make the last payment on my five hundred dollar loan before the end of the school year. It was a glorious feeling to be out of debt. I could see my chance to get back to the university, which I was able to do that fall. I wrote something like the following to my uncle, the cashier of the bank: "Enclosed is a check for the balance on my loan. It is my declaration of independence!"

In one of my first experiences selling graduation pins, the class president introduced me by announcing to the students that I represented the Tanner Company. I didn't have a company at that time, no address for a company, no desk, no stationery, not anything but a few samples of gold pins I carried in my pocket. But I didn't correct his introduction. From then on, I presented myself as a representative of the O. C. Tanner Company. Eventually my progress allowed me to buy a chair, a desk, and a letter file. With this equipment, I began to feel I was establishing myself in the world of business.

After leaving Spanish Fork, I taught for a year in the seminary at Granite High School in Salt Lake City. The next year I taught part-time at the East High School and South High School seminaries. I needed these teaching jobs, together with my jewelry sales, to help me get by as a student at the university. I was living with my mother and sister, Lois. I was glad I could help with family expenses after such a long time away on my mission and teaching in Spanish Fork.

Turning to Business in Search of Religious Independence

I have described the mostly positive experiences I had teaching seminary, but while I was teaching at East High School, the chairman of the seminary board called me in to raise objections to my liberalism. From his strictly orthodox church position, I was suspect. I innocently thought my liberalism was a true interpretation of the Mormon religion. I was quite disturbed with this interview. It was a new experience for me, and it seemed unfriendly.

In a way, it was something of a turning point in my life. I began to think more about becoming financially independent. I started to work harder in my business for I felt that, at some future time, my intellectual integrity might be at risk. I wanted to live and teach without undue pressures. I reasoned that with financial independence, I could be more assured of my freedom as a teacher in religion.

At times I felt a little self-conscious, in shifting to the role of a traveling salesman, interrupting the schedule of teachers and students in a high school. I was a teacher myself and the author of textbooks used in the seminaries. Notwithstanding my pride as a teacher and author, and feeling some reluctance in what I considered the more modest role of a traveling salesman, I pursued my goals.

Meeting the Competition

My first experience in business competition stood in stark contrast to the sheltered environment of a teacher. I made my first appointment to sell class rings at a nearby high school. I was invited by a courteous principal to his office where he introduced me to a competitor, Mr. Stickney, who was representing the T. V. Allen Company of Los Angeles. Mr. Stickney was a fine looking man who had sold that high school and other nearby schools their class rings for many years. I was told by the principal that each of us, together with representatives of other class ring companies, would be given equal time with the senior class ring committee. I felt a bit uneasy as I waited for my turn. It was my first experience in direct competition.

The atmosphere was strained. All of us would lose except one. As salesmen, we tried to be pleasant toward each other, but it was clear our friendliness was superficial. On this occasion, the decision of the committee was unanimous for Mr. Stickney. The whole experience was unpleasant for me. While my work as a teacher was hard, the atmosphere was always pleasant. Here the atmosphere was different. I had entered into a new world, the reality of business competition.

I continued to keep my appointments, however unpleasant, with other nearby high schools. Again Mr. Stickney, my strongest competitor, was always there. In each case, the ring committee gave him their order. I went on losing in competition nearly all the remainder of that school year. I found these failures very difficult, and many times I thought I would give up trying to sell class rings. Surely, I thought, there must be a better way, a more pleasant way, of earning money. But I could not bring myself to give up, and I did have some success in selling seminary pins.

At the beginning of the next school year, I thought up the idea of designing my own class rings. One design I used was a large ruby encrusted with the high school letter. In my first competition with it, I won at Provo High School, later at Lincoln High School, and then at Pleasant Grove. The manufacturer in Salt Lake now had orders for three large graduating classes. This was all his small shop could produce. I needed to find other manufacturers if I were to get more orders.

The next year, 1929, I located a truly first-rate class ring manufacturer, the Herff Jones Company of Indianapolis, Indiana. Mr. Stickney left the territory, where, as my competitor, he had been so successful. With his departure, I felt I had a better chance. I still had several other good competitors, but I became quite successful and my territory expanded to include the high schools in eastern Idaho. I added other jewelry items to my line, high school awards, club pins, etc. I overcame some of the unpleasantness associated with severe competition. The comfortable environment of a teacher was now being rivaled by success in business. I had entered upon a new way of life.

Learning the Value of Good Preparation

Sometimes when I lost the decision of the ring selection committee, students would thank me sincerely and in a friendly way tell me the vote was close. But I was all too aware that, for me, second place was the same as last. Some kinds of enterprises reward second or third place, and some losers in competition soon get a second chance. But when I lost a class ring order, a whole school year would have to pass before I would be given another chance. So when I met a class ring committee, I felt real pressure to win that day and that hour. I learned that success depended on very careful preparation.

Selling class rings required a unique approach. As I have described, several competitors would be invited to appear on the same day at the school, and each salesman was given equal time for his presentation. Occasionally I would be invited to meet with the whole class of seniors, which was an exciting experience. Besides convincing the students, I had to consider the influence of the advisor, and sometimes the principal of the high school. But then, even when I won the order, and pleased all concerned by doing a first-class job, the very next year I knew I would face new class officers, and sometimes new faculty as well.

Regrets for losing were not so painful if "no stone had been left unturned," if every conceivable preparation had been made in order to win. I continued to follow this lesson of thorough preparation when I shifted from school jewelry to corporate recognition awards. My later success with large companies may be partly attributed to these first lessons about good preparation in selling high schools.

Among other things in those first years, I carefully studied how and why people preferred various designs of jewelry. Also I learned that people can generally tell if a ring or pin has been made with great care by a skilled craftsman. I always carried a magnifying glass in a convenient pocket to help corporate executives judge the quality of my product. Also, in those early years, I became good at predicting the chances I had with a particular design or special sample. I found the best chance for winning was not necessarily in the selling itself, but in the design of the product, its originality, the harmony and sharpness of every detail, the beauty of a curved line, the contrast of colors, and so forth. I would stand for hours over a drawing board, until my feet got so tired I had to sit down. I carefully supervised others in manufacturing. With some of their failures, I learned a lot about patience. Sometimes I had to find a diplomatic way of asking a craftsman to do the job all over again. Supervision is the difficult road of every entrepreneur, particularly if the work is trying to manufacture a jewelry design that may win out in competition.

Why I Became a Manufacturer

I might say that I was practically pushed into manufacturing. I hadn't sought to become a manufacturer, but the companies that made the pins and rings I sold often disappointed me—sometimes with their late delivery, and sometimes with their inferior quality. These problems seemed insurmountable to me. I couldn't bear to disappoint my customers with poor service. I turned to manufacturing to make my job as salesman easier. To do that I had to develop a whole new kind of business. This was no small undertaking. I faced new demands— getting capital, finding a work site, training craftsmen, meeting a payroll, competing for customers, budgeting overhead expenses. These problems seemed almost overwhelming.

As a salesman I did fairly well immediately. But as a manufacturer, I had a great deal to learn. I went into partnership with Al Warren. We had our shop in the Utah Savings and Trust building. After a year, Al decided to go into business for himself. I was truly discouraged when he made this announcement. I hardly knew where to turn. Art Schuman, an engraver, generously offered to help me by taking my manufacturing equipment to his home in Salt Lake's Avenues district.

My First Employee

My first real experience as a manufacturer started when I met two former students I had taught in high school, Pearse Labrum and Wanda Hemingway. Wanda spoke quite frankly. She said, "Pearse and I would like to get married but Pearse can't find a job." This was at the time of the Great Depression. I took a moment to wish them well. Then a few weeks later, I happened to meet Pearse again. In the meantime I had collected a few materials and had made plans to open a shop in my mother's basement. I asked Pearse to help me. He was delighted to get a job.

I had learned a few things about manufacturing and now I had one employee to help me. This was Pearse's first job out of high school. We both had a lot to learn! I remember the look on Pearse's face when I gave him his first paycheck. Here was his chance to get married. And it was my first experience as a full-fledged employer. I was meeting a payroll. A new sense of mission came into my life and it has stayed with me up to the present time. Pearse continued with me for forty years and he became an excellent craftsman.

One of the first experiences Pearse and I had in manufacturing was our experiment in building a striking or drop-hammer. We installed it in mother's garage. Some of the materials we needed we found in a junk yard. One item was a railroad car axle made of solid steel. Pearse and I got a hacksaw and sawed about two feet off the axle. It must have weighed a hundred pounds. This solid piece of steel we raised with pulleys by hand and then dropped to drive the gold into the die. However, it dropped with such force and noise that eventually the neighbors complained our hammer was rattling the dishes in their cupboards. Our first work bench was an old table we repaired. We couldn't have had a more humble beginning.

After several years, we moved to a downtown location. The first year we were in the Atlas Building, then we moved to the large basement of the Capitol Theatre building. There we remained for nineteen years. But I always remember, with affection and gratitude, that my mother's dining room was my first office, her basement my first shop. Her garage provided the space for my expansion into manufacturing.

Apprenticeship

I look on the nineteen years when my company occupied the basement of the Capitol Theatre building as years of my apprenticeship in manufacturing. There was a lot to learn, but I was a fairly good student. Realizing the future of my company would depend on both selling and manufacturing, I needed competent and dedicated people with me. My nephew, Norman Tanner, helped me in selling, Lenny Hilton in manufacturing, and Sargent Streeper in management. Others joined us in time and somehow we kept things together. These nineteen years in the basement were years of mistakes, but also years when steps of learning and progress were made. There was a lot to win and a lot to lose.

It was a great day when I found a piece of land on which to construct a building that suited our needs. With our new building, we could leave the basement and look out on open skies. We no longer had to ask: "Is it raining outside?" "Is it snowing?" We could see for ourselves what the weather might be. This was a big step in our progress.

Raising Capital

There are a number of ways to raise capital—obtaining a bank loan, tapping a savings account, receiving an inheritance, reinvesting profit, etc.—but the most common method in business is to incorporate and sell stock. I raised capital by reinvesting the profit my company earned. There are risks and difficulties with this method, as with the others. Suppose the company does not earn a profit to reinvest? Suppose there is a business recession, or there is new and stronger competition? There are so many pitfalls that may limit profit. But over the years I had a measure of success.

Why did I follow this plan of reinvesting my earnings? Because I wanted to be free from the pressure of stockholders clamoring for dividends. In gaining my own capital to operate and grow, I wouldn't have to worry about dividends depleting my profits. I would also be more free to conduct my business as I saw fit. I sincerely believe that if I had sold stock, the company may not have survived. Survival was a big problem for about the first thirty years. It is difficult, if not painful, to run a business and be undercapitalized—not to be able to pay bills on time, not be able to get a bank loan, to worry about meeting the payroll. All these and other problems were part of my daily life in these early years.

Finally, a glorious time came to the O. C. Tanner Company: We began to earn a profit that was sufficient to discount our bills. We were no longer in need, or at the mercy of the bank. We began to feel more assurance in meeting severe competition. We could afford to pay better wages and I could sleep better. Eventually we were even able to pay a good annual dividend to our existing shareholders.

Ownership of the O. C. Tanner Company

During the first eleven years I owned one hundred percent of the company. Then I began to give away some of my ownership, first to key people in my company, then to family members, and finally to three universities in Utah. I did this without payment to me for the value of the stock because

I wanted to be generous to those who helped me. My next ambition was to help financially with favorite good causes while I was still alive. That dream finally came true.

In 1938, I made an agreement with my nephew, Norman Tanner, and with Newell Barlow whereby Norman could gain a twenty-percent interest in the company and Newell a ten-percent interest. Norman invested one thousand dollars in exchange for a two-percent interest. I agreed to give the remaining eighteen percent of Norman's interest and all of Newell's interest to them, in addition to their salaries, over a ten-year period of employment. In 1941, I extended the agreement to allow Pearse Labrum to receive five percent. My motive was simple: I wanted these key employees to stay with me and give their best efforts. Eventually I bought back the interests which had been given to Newell and Pearse, increased Norman's share to thirty-five percent and accelerated the transfer of my stock to him. I continued to give away my stock to family members and to three universities in Utah, until I had given away ninety-four percent of it.

There are two classes of company stock—voting and non-voting. I distributed the voting stock so that my family retained the controlling interest in the company. I did that so that we could elect the board of directors and lead the company as we thought best. To perpetuate the company and preserve its excellence, we placed our voting stock in trusts that prohibit the sale or merger of the company. I believe that this is very important to our employees and customers. Needless to say, I am very proud that the O. C. Tanner Company is now the leading company of its kind in America.

The Tanner Company's Key Idea

In 1945, after eighteen years with school and organization jewelry, I began to think about a wholly new idea. I decided to see if corporations would use emblematic awards to recognize their employees. We had been fairly successful with high schools and colleges, but each year we had to sell the order all over again. I thought executives of a corporation would be more permanent, that corporations might be more durable customers. So I began to wonder about emblematic recognition awards in industry, such as recognition awards for sales, length of service, and safety achievements.

At the time, such awards were scarcely used anywhere in America, outside of telephone and utility companies, and the emblems available were inexpensive—mostly bronze, sterling and gold filled, not designed for beauty and quality. With the prospect of such a new market, I traveled throughout the United States, meeting with corporate executives. In essence, I was trying to make the case that recognizing and motivating employees with beautiful, quality emblems would promote better employer/employee relations .

One challenge I faced was convincing people that a small company, located in Utah, could be as good in manufacturing, service, and delivery, as companies in Chicago, New York, or New England. That was not easy. Utah was a long distance away. In subsequent years, with the advent of air transport and communications technology, this problem has disappeared.

In those first years, I would travel by train to big cities with samples from my shop, make a sale, get the order approved, and then literally rush back to Salt Lake to figure out how to manufacture the product I had just sold. Each customer and each order was different. But this turned out to be a safe way of doing business, because whatever we set out to manufacture had already been sold. Accumulations of inventory were minimized. A large unsold inventory can be the Achilles' Heel of any jewelry business.

When we sold a recognition program to a corporation, we also had to help them make it successful. We had to learn much about a variety of businesses nationwide. The stakes were high. Progress added competitors, as well as customers. I enjoyed the challenge, and gave it all I had.

The War Years, 1941–45

The war years were a busy time in my life. I kept the company alive, sometimes just barely. I continued to teach at Stanford, never counting the times I commuted between Palo Alto and Salt Lake. While at Stanford, I would often catch the "City of San Francisco" at Oakland, get off in Ogden, then take a train to Salt Lake City. After a day or two with company people, I would catch the "City of San Francisco" in Ogden and be at Stanford the next morning.

Manufacturing was limited during the war years because all metals—copper, silver, and bronze—were rationed for the war effort. So I opened a chain of jewelry stores, three in Salt Lake, one in Murray, one in Tremonton, and one in Nephi. Later, to concentrate my capital and energies, I sold all but one of these stores to those people who were then managing them. I kept one store in the Capitol Theatre building, and later this store was moved to 15 South Temple, near where it stands today.

A Lesson in National Competition

Right after World War II, I learned a great lesson in competition. I was selling Western Electric in New York City. After several years of successfully selling various divisions of the Bell Telephone system, each in open competition, I thought it would be nice if I could join several of these customers into a single, three-year contract through Western Electric. With this arrangement, I would be free from the annual worry and expense of meeting competition with each particular telephone division. My motive was clearly to bypass the hard work of competing every single year for each division of Western Electric.

To achieve this, I worked out the best deal I had ever given—certainly better than any competitor had ever offered.

I attempted to sell this bargain to the officials in the home office of Western Electric, first to those at lower echelons, then to officials of a higher level, and finally to the vice-president. My offer included marked improvements in design, workmanship, and overall beauty of the emblems. For price reasons, their professional buyers were sold on my attractive proposal. The personnel department loved my improvements. Now only one person, a high official of Western Electric, stood between me and by far the largest order I had ever sold.

I waited in the lobby for the decision with great hope and with my usual anxiety. One of the lower-ranking officials brought me the decision. I could tell before he spoke that the verdict was negative. "Don't you know," he said—as if I should—"that it is our policy never to give a contract beyond one year's duration?"

"No," I replied, "no one told me about this policy." No one had objected to my sales idea, so several people, including myself, were embarrassed when we learned of this one-year time limitation. As we talked in the lobby of Western Electric's building, there on Broadway in New York City, (then one of the beautiful office buildings of the world), I leaned against one of its giant columns feeling disappointed and discouraged.

Then I learned a lesson that burned deeply into me. The Western Electric executive said, "Tanner, I might as well be frank and make one thing clear. You will have to bid every year for our business, and though you may think you have the best product, the price will determine whether you get the order." I will never forget how I felt at that moment. The official could see my disappointment, but after all, he too had been burned by allowing me to reach his boss with my contract proposal.

I was discouraged, not so much because I had lost a three-year contract, which had taken me a year to pursue, but because I now realized what my future would be. I would have to return to Salt Lake and create a manufacturing capability that could bid competitively against any and all other jewelry manufacturing companies in our industry in America. I wondered if I could do that. I was not sure. My perpetual confidence wavered just a little. But big challenges remind me of the proverb: A long journey begins with only one step. I decided to take that step.

The Risks of an Entrepreneur

The following stories from the early decades of the company's life give glimpses of a few of the risks and problems I encountered as an entrepreneur. Mostly, they are stories about surviving, about getting through the times when the company was in jeopardy.

I start with the story of a political effort to eliminate me as a salesman of class rings. It was during the worst years of the Great Depression. Jobs were lost everywhere. Any new boy on the block was unwelcome. My competitors claimed my rings were made by a company outside of Utah. They asked the Chamber of Commerce to persuade principals not to purchase rings from me because they were not made in Utah. For a time, I thought my venture might end quickly.

Later, a competitor was able to get the chairman of a fraternity jewelry committee to write a letter to his national fraternity officers, complaining about the quality of my product. The writer later admitted his letter was false, and apologized to me, but the damage had already been done. Word of the letter, or copies of it, got around to all the fraternities and sororities. That letter virtually ended my credibility in that market.

I almost hesitate to tell one very early experience. I was unable to borrow some money and I needed to make a sales trip. I tried everywhere to get a loan. Finally, I took my wife's diamond ring (with her consent) and pawned it. I could not help feeling very self-conscious in such a transaction, and the loan on the ring was humiliatingly small, at least it seemed so to me. I was glad to redeem it as soon as I could.

Not long afterward, a lawyer asked me to come to his office and talk about my poor credit rating. He attempted to get me to sell my business to one of his clients. The alternative, he suggested, would be a foreclosure, forcing me into an unpleasant bankruptcy. I was shocked; it seemed like blackmail.

At one point I decided to manufacture special jewelry orders for stores to sell. This effort failed because all six of the craftsmen in my shop at the time joined together and quit just prior to Christmas. Their timing cost me many of my customers. It was a rather bleak holiday for me.

Bad faith actions have always surprised me. Many years ago, one of my salesmen forged my name to a title that cost me the possession of my car. I badly needed that car, and so I was quite upset. This was my first experience with outright dishonesty.

Another serious time for me came when my former sales manager was hired by one of our competitors. His assignment was to hire key artists, salesmen, and craftsmen away from the Tanner Company. I appealed to the Federal Trade Commission that this competitor had acted in restraint of trade. Testimony was given in a federal hearing in Chicago, and I finally won my case, but through the years of appeals and hearings our company had been seriously damaged. I think our competitor believed he had ended the life of the O. C. Tanner Company.

Once I found the company had expanded too rapidly and I couldn't meet a delinquent federal excise tax bill of sixty thousand dollars. When I received a demand for payment, I went to see the chief of the Internal Revenue Service for Utah. He sympathetically listened to my story and my promises, and gave me a year and a half extension to get the delinquent tax paid—with penalties of course. I recall he told me such a favor would never be repeated. At the time my capital situation was very critical, but I was able to keep the agreement with the IRS.

In the early years my financial statements often worried bank officials. Changing banks was sometimes more or less involuntary. I will never forget how relieved I felt when I so desperately needed a loan and one bank was willing to make it. I felt like kissing the cornerstone of the bank building as I passed by!

Of all the difficulties in an entrepreneurial enterprise, the most unpleasant is not having enough money to pay bills on time. Sometimes I really suffered, though I always knew I exacerbated this situation by trying to expand without sufficient capital.

One experience had as much comedy as tragedy. When I opened my first jewelry store on Main Street, I bought a second-hand safe. I put all the expensive items in the safe before going home at night. The next morning I was unable to open the door. There was a defect in the lock combination. It took me two days to finally get the door open. I employed an expert with a blow torch. He put canvas over the windows, hoping passersby would not think we were robbing the store. Smoke was everywhere. All my expensive jewelry was inside the vault. By the time I got the door open, the heat of the blow torch had melted the boxes and ruined some of the jewelry. When I arrived home late that night, Grace wondered what made me look so tired and dirty.

On the other hand, the life of an entrepreneur is not so bad, when one can see light at the end of the tunnel. I was restless with my dreams of expansion. There were many more near-disasters than those mentioned here, but we survived. I took risks I doubt I would like to take again.

A Fire that Destroyed Our Shop

A different kind of crisis occurred on the fourth of July, 1946. Early that morning I was aroused by a telephone call. A voice told me there was a serious fire raging in the Capitol

Theatre building. I hurried down to find several fire trucks and a large crowd of people. The fire had started in the basement adjoining my shop. The elevator shaft acted as a draft, and flames were coming out of a window on the third floor. I could see it was a large fire and damage would be considerable. When the fire was extinguished, the basement had several inches of standing water on the floor. Great damage had been done to my benches, files, and desks, both from the fire and the water. About all that could be salvaged were our steel dies. Water and fire could not damage them, but if they should rust, the dies could lose their value. This was a big worry, and several wonderful employees pitched in with great energy. The dies were loaded into boxes and taken to our garage at home where they could be cleaned. They were wiped free of moisture and Vaseline was put on them to prevent rusting. Even my small children helped. Although I did have some fire insurance, I never fully recovered my loss. We simply cleaned up the basement and started over again.

My shop had been pretty well destroyed. We learned that the fire had started because ushers from the theatre used one of the theatre basement rooms to smoke cigarettes. We learned also that one usher was unable to get out of the basement and died from asphyxiation. I attended his funeral. The fact that a young man could lose his life so quickly made a lasting impression on me.

A Union Drive

Perhaps the most emotional problem in the life of the Tanner Company came when an attempt was made to unionize the employees. It caught me completely by surprise. Up to that time I had never given any thought to the possibility of unionization. As I drove my car off the company parking lot one day, two men stopped me and one of them handed me a leaflet. It was given to all employees of the company as they were leaving the plant. The handout was a crude drawing of me and contained comments to the effect that I was the unfeeling and selfish owner of the O. C. Tanner Company. Little did I realize at the time that this union drive would last for more than three years, from 1961 until November 30, 1964.

Psychologically, I was unprepared for it. For thirty-three years I had known all my employees by their first names. We seemed to have a mutual respect, and with many I had a warm friendship. Now there was a division between those who favored a union and those who did not. This difference of opinion became sharper as the days, weeks, months, and years passed. Some of my oldest employees stopped speaking to me and, with others, any greeting was strictly formal. Some remained respectful and loyal but there were few smiles. The drive for a union was so intense that we became divided among ourselves; there were hard feelings.

It was unlawful, under the National Labor Relations Act, for any representative of a company, during a drive for union membership, to say anything to an employee that might be construed as a promise or a threat. I found it easy to comply with that law, since I agreed that an attempt to influence people with a promise or a threat would be intimidating and undignified. I remained silent during those long years, although to the company management I did express my view that some companies may be helped by a union, and some companies may be hurt by one. I still hold this view.

In our company every order we receive is won by competitive bidding. If we were compelled to bid at higher prices, we could easily lose our market share. Knowing first hand how good our competitors were, I have always said, and still maintain, that "our orders are hard to win and easy to lose." Moreover, the Tanner Company sells *time delivery,* that is, awards must reach a company in time for an employee's anniversary date. If there were a strike, most of the O. C. Tanner Company customers would be lost within a very short time. A delay in making a delivery date would have a domino effect on all our shipments. Competitors located nearer our customers, would certainly step in to take advantage of any on-time delivery problems we might have.

The union organizers, who held meetings in employees' homes and in nearby cafes, had to have a majority of the employees vote to unionize the company. The voting was secret and supervised by the National Labor Relations Board. The union lost the first election by a margin of two to one. The following year, with an even stronger union drive, the union lost again, this time by a narrower margin, about three to two.

A year later a third vote was scheduled. I thought the union might win this time. It seemed to me that there was more ill will than goodwill, more animosity by far than friendliness. There was no way of negotiating, no reason to hope for loyalty, just stony silence and sharp glances. Such an atmosphere had been unknown at the Tanner Company before the union drive. During this period, I thought to myself, as I met my employees each day, "You keep your dignity and I'll keep mine." But the wide distance between us—this suspicion and coolness—was not the way I wanted to live with the people of my company.

Occasionally a cold rebuff or chilly rumor made me wonder if this was to be a permanent condition of the company. The wear and tear began to tell on me. I thought of options— selling the company or turning over its management to someone else. But if I were to mention such thoughts, and if I were quoted, it could easily be construed as an illegal threat or a promise. This would amount to an unfair labor practice and the law would automatically install the union. Complete silence was not my disposition, but silent I had to remain, both by law and by personal choice. It was a new experience for me. I was not born to live with this kind of antagonism, which was one reason I chose not to practice law. A future of adversarial relationships in my business was not for me.

Then on the eve of the third election, to my great surprise, the union organizers decided they did not have enough votes to win, and so canceled the election. Although this result was better than I expected, the union then filed a complaint against the company, alleging that it had engaged in unfair labor practices.

Their case included affidavits from any and all people who had ever worked for me and been unhappy about the way they were treated. If they could show a single unfair labor practice by me, the need for an election would be circumvented and a union could automatically be installed. I was not acquainted with the workings of the National Labor Relations Board until I became embroiled in this two-year controversy, first in Salt Lake City, then Denver, and finally, before the full board in Washington, D.C. I was certain that during so many years, I must have made mistakes in my dealings with people, mistakes that the NLRB would uncover.

But early in December of 1964, I received a letter dated November 30, signed by Irving M. Herman, Director of Appeals, from the Office of the General Counsel to the National Labor Relations Board. His letter reviewed each of the several allegations of unfair labor practices. In each charge, the board concluded I was not guilty. One can imagine how pleased I was. I had passed a critical test. It seemed almost too good to be true. I doubt if any diploma ever meant so much as that letter meant to me.

Our Factories, Offices, and Showcase Store

As I mentioned earlier, in 1954 I bought a piece of land and built my first factory. The land was formerly occupied by the greenhouses of the Salt Lake Floral Company. I bought it for a reasonable price, and sold most of it to the Surety Life Insurance Company and the World Motel. The profit from the sale of these two pieces of land gave me enough capital to start building a new factory. The original structure was ninety feet by ninety feet. That was all I could afford at the time. My bank refused me a loan to help construct the building, but I took a chance. It was a thrill, after almost twenty years in the basement of the Capitol Theatre building, to move my company to its present location at 1930 South State Street.

There is a lot of personal satisfaction in building a business. It might be akin to what an artist feels when painting a picture, or a composer when writing a musical score. Today, our recent expansion is now complete. We have a total factory floor space of over 340,000 square feet, and about twenty-two acres for parking, offices, and manufacturing.

We also have a fine manufacturing plant in Burlington, near Toronto, Canada. Prior to its establishment, we had sold many accounts in Canada, but the duty for importing goods put us in a weakened competitive position. Finally we decided to build our own plant there, expand our sales, and avoid the disadvantage of having to pass the import duty costs on to our customers (this plan being formed and implemented before the NAFTA agreement). This has turned out to be a successful venture. Our method of establishing the plant was simply to transfer, from Salt Lake City to Canada, people who had the necessary skills, so they could train the Canadians we hired to work in the Burlington plant. Today there is a team of nearly one hundred people working for O. C. Tanner Manufacturing Limited, a wholly owned subsidiary. Sales have increased every year since we opened the plant.

When the Kennecott Building was constructed on the corner of South Temple and Main Street, I had a great opportunity to build a jewelry store at the ground level. I hoped it would be America's most beautiful store. To build it, I sent a team of people to many of the major cities in the United States and Europe, including New York, Dallas, Atlanta, Boston, Paris, and London, to scout for ideas. These representatives and sales people were to meet together and review what seemed to them ideas worth incorporating. The store was built and has recently been remodeled. I think it still holds first place in terms of beauty.

A Sense of Accomplishment

At the supper table I would occasionally hear my mother say thoughtfully: "Well, I've accomplished a lot today." Then she would recall her accomplishments, such as washing done, jars of fruit put up for winter, floors cleaned, clothes mended, something fixed. Sometimes her list included a lonely neighbor visited, or some food she had given to someone in need.

Sometimes I have followed mother's example of listing things I had accomplished at the end of the day, or things I hoped to accomplish at the beginning of the day. I spend most of my Saturdays and Sundays trying to solve some new problem. Problems I face as an entrepreneur always seem new to me, their number and variety infinite. Sometimes the problem is a small one, such as where to place a new work bench, but there are thornier problems too and people problems are the most difficult for me.

In any case people who work with me are accustomed to a comment I often make first thing in the morning: "Now about our decision yesterday, I think we should scrap it for a new and still better idea." In fact, my employees have often said, "We knew you would make some change, so we have delayed carrying out yesterday's decision." I will always be relieved to hear that I am not too late to try for a better solution.

Creating Jobs

In the summer of 1993 I called on my friend Professor H. L. A. Hart at his home in Oxford. It was to be our last visit for he died later that year. Professor Hart was one of the world's great scholars in jurisprudence, yet he had a realistic approach to life. At one point in our conversation, he asked me what I most enjoyed doing, what I thought I could do best. It was a big question and I gave what I thought was a rather awkward answer. I said, "I think I am good as an employer." Then I added my reason, "I find I am able to get on well with people."

His reply made my visit memorable. He looked at me and his face seemed to light up with a smile, "Yes," he said, "I think that is good. I like that." I shall always remember these encouraging words. A great scholar, Oxford's professor of jurisprudence, had expressed appreciation for my role as an employer. It gave me a pleasant moment of satisfaction that I haven't forgotten.

Creating jobs is a way to help people help themselves, providing paychecks to warm a house, educate children, purchase security or amenities. In any case, it may be the major accomplishment of my eighty-nine years. It is surely one I feel good about.

Better Employee Relations

As for the Tanner Company's work, I sometimes reflect that we put a drop of oil on the bearings of the free enterprise system. We help companies run a little more smoothly, with a little less friction, cultivating a more friendly environment where people work. Thus, what we offer are not only achievement awards, but friendly and beautiful occasions where the giver may be as pleased as the one who receives.

One might say we deal in two values—the value of beauty and the value of kindness. We supply the beauty, and our customers supply the kindness. Kindness is expressed in a company's desire to recognize and honor its people. After all, giving the productive years of one's life, most of the daylight hours of each working day, is a huge sacrifice. Beautiful awards inspire a high morale and better performance. Each year three million Tanner awards are presented to the employees of companies located throughout the world. A great many changes have taken place since I began to sell recognition awards. American industry is now being reengineered to meet world competition. We are pleased to be a part of such improvements.

Two Generations

Many wonderful people helped me build the O. C. Tanner Company. My sixty-six years with them equal about two generations. As I look back, some were skilled craftsman, some successful in sales, and some gifted in management. I would like to pay tribute to four of the key people who I think of as the first generation of Tanner Company employees.

Pearse Labrum was the very first. Together we opened a jewelry shop in the basement of my mother's home. He worked with me for forty years. Norman Tanner, my oldest brother's son, started working for me in 1937. With his cheerful disposition and friendly personality, Norman made important contributions in sales. He retired in 1981 after forty-four years of service, but continues to serve as a member of the board of directors. Sargent Streeper was a friend going back to high school and college days. A man of good humor and great brilliance, he gave me good advice in my search for able people. Sarge passed away on January 19, 1985. We all miss him. Lenny Hilton came "up from the ranks" as an excellent shop foreman. He had good common sense and was very loyal for all forty-nine years he worked with me. I thought of him as a diamond in the rough who became a polished gem.

Turning now to the second generation of leaders, I am fortunate to have found many gifted people on whom I rely as the company grows. One I work with closely is my daughter, Carolyn Tanner Irish, chair-elect. She has in some way been a part of the company all her life. She shares my hopes and plans for the perpetuation and future success of the Tanner

Company. Carolyn has served as a member of the board of directors since 1979. She has a brilliant mind, superb judgment, and great leadership ability.

Don Ostler, CEO of the Tanner Company, is a man of sterling character and outstanding leadership. Don and I have worked together like a team of horses pulling on the same doubletrees. In 1991, Don, Carolyn, and I chose Kent Murdock, a successful Salt Lake lawyer, to be our new president. He has more than fulfilled our expectations.

Others who make invaluable contributions to our leadership team include Bill Paul, who has directed our sales efforts for twenty-five years; Lowell Benson, our executive vice-president, who has many roles in the company, including diamond and gold purchasing; Kaye Jorgensen, a woman of unfailing strength and grace, who is vice-president of human resources; and Brent Evans, our very able senior vice-president of manufacturing. Many other talented and dedicated management people help guide the O. C. Tanner Company in all of its operations. We also have forty-eight regional sales offices located in the principal cities of the United States and Canada. Our sales people are extremely able, energetic, and independent.

The board of directors includes four "outside" directors, people of broad experience, great wisdom and public spirit: Dallin H. Oaks, formerly chair of the board of PBS, president of Brigham Young University, and now an apostle in the LDS church; Chase N. Peterson, formerly vice-president of Harvard University and president of the University of Utah, now on the medical school faculty there; Stephen D. Nadauld, formerly dean of the BYU Business School, and president of Weber State University, now a general authority in the LDS church; Rex E. Lee, formerly Solicitor General of the United States, now president of Brigham Young University. Together with Kent, Carolyn, and my grandson, Stephen Irish, an honors graduate of Stanford University, they will work to find and train future generations of leaders for the company.

Celebrating

In 1987 the company celebrated its sixtieth anniversary. The celebration took place in Salt Lake City's Symphony Hall. Over three thousand guests were present to enjoy "An Evening of Music," performed by the Utah Symphony, the Utah Opera, and the Mormon Tabernacle Choir. I tried to speak for the company:

> The Tanner Company is a group of people who love this beautiful city. Each of us wants to earn his or her own way. We want to be independent, have our own homes, be free to make personal choices, create a life that can be glad and beautiful and good.
>
> To do this we have created a company that makes recognition awards, presented by companies to their own people who are located throughout the world. Many corporations send their representatives to Salt Lake to look us over. They are favorably impressed.
>
> In our vocation of designing and manufacturing, as artisans and craftsmen, as secretaries and sales people, we strive to make ourselves a cut above the average. We try to do this with a few simple rules:
>
> - We do not overpromise, we keep our word.
> - We combine efficiency with friendliness.
> - We enjoy living while we earn our living.

Balance

I have always been attracted to the Greek ideals of balance, harmony, right proportion, nothing-in-excess. They are not always or immediately helpful to an entrepreneurial enterprise. I find, however, that this enterprise did assist me toward them personally. Business provided, for me, a whole different perspective on the world than what I had gained through my religious and philosophical vocations. The latter in turn helped to make my company much more than just another enterprise. All, together, have given me a life of daily excitement and extraordinary satisfaction.

Chapter Eight

PUBLIC SERVICE AND SHARING

. . .

Chapter Eight

PUBLIC SERVICE AND SHARING

A gentleman's agreement with life

is to put more back than we take out.

—Professor Luccock

• • •

Introduction

My professional life was divided between teaching and business. Beyond that, I became involved with other interests such as the United Nations, a symphony hall, amphitheatres, fountains, gardens, philosophy libraries, and a fine lectureship. I tried to put more back than I took out, and I loved helping when I could. Of course, the people of my company helped in much of my giving. They share in this important part of my life.

This chapter is a little difficult to write. Perhaps it is better when giving is anonymous, but I love to recall moments of giving and sharing. When I left Stanford, I dreamed I could build a company that would allow me to help with causes I cared about. It was a dream that came true, and so my last years are filled with happiness. It is indeed more blessed to give than receive.

United Nations

The major political interest of my life has been to support the United Nations. This interest is rooted in my early, though indirect, experiences of war. When I was twelve years old, the United States entered World War I. Troop trains would stop for a few minutes in Farmington to take on water and pick up recruits on their way to military training and, eventually, to France.

I recall the gathering of many people at the railroad station, and the excitement of the approaching troop train. Newly inducted soldiers were dressed neatly in khaki uniforms, wearing wide-brimmed hats and leggings. The soldiers' parents and friends were present to say farewell. Sometimes a church choir or a band was there. Before the train arrived, there was often a speech by the mayor, bishop, or both. Many were crying. It was a child's first view of problems beyond his own community. Such farewells made a lasting impression on me.

Later, while serving a mission in Germany for the LDS church, I visited many homes of German people who had lost their loved ones in that war. One evening, a Mormon convert in Germany told me that he had been a soldier manning a machine gun in the front-line trenches. "The American soldiers came at us standing straight up," he related graphically. "We would mow them down, then retreat, but they kept on coming. Soon they learned to drop down when we opened fire. I have no idea how many my machine gun killed," he said, "but I still remember this experience with a vividness that sometimes wakes me at night."

After I was released from my mission, my travels included a tour of the battlefields around Verdun. In a very short period of time, more than 600 thousand men on both sides had been killed there. That awesome experience of walking through the battlefields helped form my resolve to do what I could to avoid such tragedy.

In the early 1940s I was assistant chaplain at Stanford University, and war again touched my life. My sermons were often concerned with reconciling war and the Christian religion. I recall one argument: "How can you believe in God with this war going on?" The believer replies, "When I think of Hitler, I could not believe in God if this war were not going on."

These and other experiences helped form my commitment to make the United Nations successful. It was a loyalty
I felt from the first day the charter was signed in San Francisco
in 1945. We wanted the conference table to replace the battle-
field. Failing this, in a nuclear age, the consequence might
be no world at all. On behalf of the United Nations, I traveled to many parts of the world. During the early Cold War
years in conservative Salt Lake City, I was sometimes called
"Mr. United Nations," and though I was aware that such a title
was a cold compliment in that climate, my devotion to the
United Nations has never waivered.

The first years of my life were lived at the crest of twentieth-century optimism. During the nineteenth and first part
of the twentieth centuries, people believed education could
solve all our problems. If a problem was difficult, only more
education was needed. World War I dampened some of this
confidence, and then after World War II, pessimism (or perhaps
realism) began to pervade our thinking. We were no longer
so sure that all we needed was more education. Nevertheless, and whether justified or not, the optimism that prevailed
in my youth and early years has stayed with me, even up to the
present.

The family of nations has been divided in many ways.
Divisions are created by physical barriers—oceans, rivers,
mountains, deserts, forests—and by religions—Judaism, Christianity, Islam, Buddhism, Hinduism, Shintoism, Zoroastri-
anism, Judaism, Sikhism, Confucianism, not to mention the
spiritual traditions of various native peoples. Other divisions
result from racial and ethnic differences, variant ideologies
and political systems, and economic and social factors. People
are educated and uneducated, literate and illiterate, scien-
tific and superstitious.

If these differences and divisions were not enough to
make peace difficult, the baser elements of human nature—
love of power, pleasure, greed—these make world peace
almost impossible. In addition, there are pockets of deep hatred

throughout the world, antagonisms brought about by past wars and atrocities. The ever-present threat of non-nuclear nations becoming nuclear reminds us of the risk of holocaust. Two universal, interacting motivations in human beings are the love of power and the love of freedom. Either can lead to war, as each side believes it is the champion of freedom, and each side wants to keep its power and become even more powerful.

I was not in San Francisco when the United Nations charter was signed by the world powers in 1945, but I was there in spirit with millions, if not most of the human race. The general principal of the United Nations stirs most everyone. "Since wars are made in the minds of men, it is in the minds of men that the foundations for peace must be laid." I became committed to working for attitudes favorable to world peace.

The most active part of my public life was directed toward strengthening the UN through education. To this end, I gave much of my time and means, traveling to Geneva and other cities of the world. In Utah, during the Cold War years, I think I spoke to nearly every group in the state—social clubs, civic associations, churches, business organizations, political parties, and others.

When a local chapter to support the United Nations was formed in Salt Lake City, I was present. We met in the Mormon Tabernacle on Temple Square and the Episcopal Bishop Arthur W. Moultan became our president. It was the belief of many that the earlier League of Nations had failed in part because of the lack of grass roots support. We thought that should not happen again. With others I labored for the United Nations organization, providing information about problems faced by all the nations. But Cold War antagonism made grass roots support for the UN very difficult to obtain.

In the late 1950s, our local organization nearly died. Utah's governor opposed the UN, as did other political and religious leaders. To defend it at that time called one's patriotism into question. I always suspected that when I assumed the presidency of the Utah organization, it was because no one else would take the job. We held monthly meetings, mostly attended by women who shared my deep convictions about peace and war. We had to dig deep to find within ourselves the strength that could support the UN. I found mine in religious and political idealism. Since nuclear war was simply unthinkable, communism had to be endured with patience. We had to remind ourselves that behind their ideologies, the people in communist countries were human beings much the same as ourselves. They wanted to survive as we did. We had to learn respect, and practice love.

During the years of the Cold War, I attended many meetings of the American Association of the United Nations (AAUN) in New York (later called the United Nations Association of the United States of America, or UNA/USA). I was on the board of governors of that organization, and I remain on the American Council of UNA/USA. In these meetings I was associated with distinguished people—Mrs. Eleanor Roosevelt, Paul Hoffman, Clark Eichelberger, Oscar de Lima, Herman Steinkraus, and many others.

Each year the World Federation of the United Nations Associations (WFUNA) convened in Geneva. I was one of five American delegates meeting with representatives from other United Nations associations throughout the world. Our offices were in Geneva, but we sometimes held our plenary sessions in other cities—Brussels, New Delhi, Monrovia, Moscow, and New York.

At the beginning of my work as a United States delegate in Geneva, I found the challenges very difficult. Communist delegates took every opportunity to slander the United States. I wanted to answer them in the same spirit, as an adversary, but I soon realized such verbal conflict would get us nowhere. I again had to search within to find resources I could bring to such an international conference, especially in face-to-face meetings with articulate communist delegates. They were skilled, confident, and persistent in presenting their arguments, and I felt hesitant, awkward, and intimidated. I was very conscious of my limited background. Though I had led an eclectic life, I was now in contact with delegates from all over the world, some of them judges and diplomats, and most of them much more experienced in public life than I.

Finally, however, after several years of these meetings in Geneva, I found peace within myself. I came to realize that notwithstanding my inexperience and their hostility, I was sustained by the major ideas of western civilization, the life of reason from ancient Greece, and the values of the Judeo-Christian tradition. I had been trained in the law, philosophy, and religion. I learned that I could speak with some understanding of world problems because, in many ways, I believed that the human condition was much the same everywhere. My basic assumption was that we had more in common with the communists than we had in our differences, and so I decided I would try to make friends with everyone.

In 1956, I was one of the first admitted to travel in the USSR. When I returned, Utahns were curious about our potential enemy. I tried to help my fellow citizens come to grips with Cold War issues. Deep suspicion was everywhere. While we had no simple answers, I was always hoping and searching for possible solutions, and I encouraged others to do the same.

Beginning in the early 1960s, the U.S. State Department sometimes asked me to host visitors from the Soviet Union. I often took them to see the Kennecott copper mine a few miles southwest of Salt Lake City. On the way back, I once pointed to the houses in Copperton, and told my visitors they were the homes of workers at the mine. I could tell they didn't believe me. With a hint of calling my bluff, he said, "It would be nice if we could visit one of these homes."

"Sure," I replied, pulling off the highway onto one of the streets in Copperton.

"May we choose which house?" one of them asked.

"Yes, I'll knock on the door. Would this one be all right?" I asked as I rolled to a stop.

"No, make it the third house after we cross the third street," said my very suspicious friend.

I became exacting that they tell me which was the third house after the third street crossing. When they agreed on the house, I knocked on the door. A middle-aged woman answered.

"Madam," I explained, "I have three communists in my car and they want to see your home. Would you be kind enough to invite them in?"

At first she stared at my car parked at the curb, then looked at me very carefully. I expected her answer to be negative. Then she smiled. "I think I know who you are," she said. "Many years ago you taught my sister in the Spanish Fork LDS seminary."

I was greatly relieved and waved her invitation to my friends. These professors of economics at the University of Moscow spent two or three hours asking questions and writing copious notes on every detail of a miner's wage and how it was spent. What pleased me most were the piano and other musical instruments in her living room. All her children took music lessons. I was pleased because I was aware my visitors were certain the Soviet Union had a corner on the best in cultural life. Our hostess made a star witness for the free enterprise system. They carefully compared their notes on the way back to Salt Lake and my impression was that they were surprised with this experience, seeing the difference between what they had been led to believe about capitalism, and what they now witnessed at first hand.

For many it is hard to recall what it was like to live with the fears and misunderstanding of the Cold War and McCarthyism. We are fortunate that this period has come to an end. We still need a strong United Nations, however, for great challenges to world peace remain. More than ever our security must be collective, and the United Nations is our best chance. Americans are now more willing to join with other nations to work toward peace. The monolithic political structure of communism has crumbled and new hopes for freedom, justice, and peace, are emerging and must be encouraged.

In October 1978, I was honored to receive the United Nations Peace Medal presented by Francis O. Wilcox from New York. He represented the United Nations Association of the United States of America. It is one of the most prized awards I have received.

Symphony Hall

One day in April of 1972, I happened to meet Governor Calvin L. Rampton. We paused to exchange greetings. He asked if I had any free time, and I quickly replied in the negative, fearful that he might have some big assignment. A governor always has many projects under consideration, and always a need for volunteers to carry them out.

"I thought you might be willing to help get a symphony hall," he explained.

"That's different," I answered. And it was different! I instantly gave him an affirmative answer, though I little dreamed the extent of what would be involved. Nor did Governor Rampton, for as he sensed my misgivings he added, "It won't take more than four hours a week." That estimate of time may have been the record understatement in his three terms as governor.

I was by this time contemplating retirement from teaching at the University of Utah. I planned to write a book and launch a considerable expansion of the O. C. Tanner Company. But a new symphony hall? My personal plans receded as I pondered this dazzling opportunity.

The building of a symphony hall in Salt Lake was a challenge that involved many people and lasted seven years, from 1972 through 1979. For many years the Mormon church generously allowed the use of the Tabernacle for symphony concerts. Renowned orchestras and famous artists enjoyed performing in that historic building. But as the popularity of the Utah Symphony required more performances and as the Mormon church wanted to use the Tabernacle for other purposes, the need for a symphony hall had become more apparent. Over the next three or four years I met with many people attracted to the idea of a new symphony hall. We had various motives and backgrounds, but our love of great music was a bond that held us together.

Music, especially classical music, has virtually a religious importance to me. My older brother, Sheldon, was a gifted pianist, and as a child I sat for long periods listening to him play. Later, as I traveled over much of the world, especially Europe, the evenings nearly always found me in a concert hall or attending an opera. So I had visited and enjoyed music in many beautiful buildings, both in America and abroad, and I had for years wanted to participate in creating such a place in Utah.

I have always believed our community can and will support it, even without relinquishing the great concert tradition of the Tabernacle. To that end Grace and I have endowed what we call, "A Gift of Music," performed jointly by the Utah Symphony Orchestra and the Mormon Tabernacle Choir. A concert is given every two years in the Tabernacle and is free to the public. One concert featuring Kiri Te Kanawa was recorded by PBS and rebroadcast on the past several Easter Sundays as "An Easter Gift of Music."

In any case it was Governor Rampton's thought that the best way for Utah to celebrate the two hundredth anniversary of our American democracy, July 4, 1976, would be to build a symphony hall. This was the idea he expressed to me in April of 1972, four years before that bicentennial year. To facilitate this connection between the local symphony hall and the national celebration, he asked me to be chairman of Utah's Bicentennial Commission.

I agreed, but only gradually did I realize that I had accepted a considerable responsibility. I was both honored and humbled by this appointment. For years I had taught a course in social ethics and one on the philosophy of democracy. Here was an opportunity to work with my fellow citizens and share with them some of the major ideals of our history, the meaning of two hundred years of a free democracy. Thus I was deeply moved by this assignment even apart from the practical task of building a symphony hall. Valuable suggestions for the overall celebration were made by many Utah leaders. I felt a growing confidence that I could do a good job in coordinating the bicentennial. I was pleased with this opportunity to express my love of country.

When I accepted this assignment, there was the possibility that Congress might appropriate 1.25 billion dollars to be divided equally, among the fifty states, each state deciding its own way of celebrating the bicentennial. Utah's share would be 25 million dollars. Congress appointed a federal bicentennial commission and that commission had retained the services of the reputable lawfirm of Booze, Allen, and Hamilton. Their job was to see that each state completed a feasibility study prior to receiving the money. Mine was to see this done for Utah.

Looking back over that first year, with all the luncheons, breakfasts, and special meetings with different leaders of the community—political, religious, civic, educational, and artistic—I came to see that having 25 million dollars to spend in Utah could get a lot of people excited. And I was one of them! Together we carefully prepared our study.

But the balloon burst when, in 1973, Congress suddenly decided the bicentennial celebration should be entirely local; that is, each state and each community within each state would have to plan and pay for its own celebration. Only 45 thousand dollars in federal money was granted to Utah. And even this amount had strings attached, namely, that before it could be distributed, it had to be matched with state money. With no money and only discouraged volunteers, dreams of the concert hall were truly diminished.

Yet I realized that our expectation of a federal grant had stirred up great interest and awareness of our need for a symphony hall. While our dreams seemed to be fading in this first year, a real core of interest had developed. With our display of charts and the designs already obtained, later work for a symphony hall would be easier.

In 1973 Governor Rampton appointed a twenty-five member Bicentennial Commission for Utah. The commission was composed of outstanding citizens from every walk of life, with broad representation of the state's minority and majority groups. Governor Rampton suggested that some of the existing state treasury surplus might be used for a concert hall. A generous legislature agreed. That year they appropriated 8 million dollars to the bicentennial commission, 6.5 million of it to be used for a concert hall, with the stipulation that it be matched by other than state money. We were now back in business. We met a countless number of times in our commission office on the fourth floor of the Capitol building.

However, another setback was a decision by the legislature to place a time limit on their offer of money. The deadline for securing matching funds was December 31, 1975. If not matched by that time, the 6.5 million dollars would return to the state treasury. We had no other option; it had to be an all-or-nothing effort on a risky general obligation bond election. We set the date for the bond election—December 16, 1975.

At that time it did not look promising. This had been a year of business recession, and worse perhaps, a year of rapid inflation. A Salt Lake County bond election, which included a concert hall, had failed in 1973. Also there was the general concern that many, perhaps most, people did not care for symphonic music, and so would vote against the bond. One private poll showed that a majority of voters did not believe the LDS church would refuse the Utah Symphony the use of the Tabernacle, so why build a new building? We were not aware that during 1975, ninety-three percent of all bond elections throughout the United States were being defeated. I recall that while my close friends were considerate and gentle, a good number were pessimistic. They had grave doubts about the bond election's chance for success. Others I knew simply did not want the bond election to be successful. They were honestly opposed to it.

I approached the election as I did any business challenge. In business, able people are important. At least they are the ones with whom we have our best chances. So I began looking for strong leadership that could win a bond election. I needed two leaders, one as general chairman, the other an executive director who would serve full time and pull all the needed elements together day by day. I found the two I needed in Jack Gallivan and Richard Eyre, and I know that without the enthusiasm of both of them, we would never have won the bond election.

In February of 1975, I first met with Richard Eyre in Washington, D.C. I sensed he wanted to return to Salt Lake City, and I offered to pay his family's moving expenses and a good year's salary if he would return and work for the bond election. In my enthusiasm, I offered to pay him an attractive bonus if the bond election turned out successfully. I really wanted to win. Accepting this offer, he did return to Utah and went to work.

To Mr. Eyre goes the credit of conceiving the idea of remodeling the Capitol Theatre as part of the bicentennial celebration. I sent him on tours of theatres and concert halls throughout the United States. On one of his trips he learned of a remodeled theatre in St. Louis that was very successful. After this experience, he tells of glancing at the Capitol Theatre as he drove down Second South, and at that moment the idea was born. He parked his car, explored the building, and within a short time was in my office full of enthusiasm. The pieces began to come together favorably. We discovered, among other things, the public relations value of preserving a great historical building. This got us a lot of favorable votes for a symphony hall, and getting such votes was our primary goal.

The second person, the general chairman of the campaign, was even more important and certainly more difficult to find. This individual had to be an esteemed citizen, widely known and able to command broad public support. The chairman had the problem and challenge of—among other things—selecting a blue-ribbon committee of highly respected citizens able to help in the general campaign.

In the search for such a general chairman, I held a number of meetings with distinguished citizens who had a particular interest in the symphony, including Milton Weilenmann, Wendell Ashton, and others. Then one day in June of 1975, Mr. Ashton suggested John W. (Jack) Gallivan, and I instantly agreed. We felt he might accept if Governor Rampton asked him. He did and Jack accepted. I felt, almost for the first time, a genuine optimism. Jack Gallivan, the publisher of the *Salt Lake Tribune,* is a great community leader, with a brilliant mind and a good heart. And, I want to add, he is my friend. With Gallivan leading a panel of distinguished citizens and Eyre's expertise as their executive director, the team was complete. Our chances for winning the bond election looked favorable, but we still had a lot of campaigning to do.

One other factor that contributed to our success (and without which we might have failed) was the help of Nathan Eldon Tanner, a member of the First Presidency of the Church of Jesus Christ of Latter-day Saints. I regard President Tanner as one of the great men I have known. His concern for the public interest, his sense of life's finest values, and his almost unerring ability to pick up the main point in a discussion were just a few of his great qualities. If I were to name the one whose help meant the most to me personally when I was chairman of the Utah Bicentennial Commission, it would be Nathan Eldon Tanner.

The day of the bond election some of us met in the Capitol Theatre to hear the returns: Maestro Maurice Abravanel, the Utah Symphony conductor; Willam Christensen, founder of Ballet West; Wendell Ashton, president of the symphony board; Herold L. Gregory, manager of the symphony; our wives; and a host of other artists, enthusiasts, spouses, and friends. The vote was 32,932 in favor and 25,716 against. We all began shaking hands and hugging each other.

I thought to myself, "Thank goodness, an election is final!" It seemed almost too good to be true—no more delays, no urgent meetings, no repeated postponements, and no appeals that could reverse the decision—just a clean, clear victory.

Ted Wilson, then mayor of Salt Lake City, told me about a convention in Boston, gathering mayors of cities about the size of Salt Lake. The chairman of this group wanted to know how Salt Lake City had been successful in passing a bond election concerning music, when bond elections to meet such basic needs as public sanitation and education had been defeated. Mayor Wilson was called to the podium for an explanation. He had not been aware of the intensity of our drive for a symphony hall and simply told them that the reason for our successful bond election was that people in Salt Lake loved symphony music. Some of those in the audience just smiled.

Georgius Y. Cannon, one of Utah's ablest architects, was retained to advise us. We were also fortunate to obtain the services of Cyril Harris of New York, one of the world's ranking acousticians, especially noted for his achievements in designing concert halls. The architectural firm of Robert Fowler and Associates designed the new building. Stephen Baird was the architect retained to remodel the Capitol Theatre. I felt that a big victory had been won. We had obtained the money, and now the specialists could do their work.

The rewards of public service are many and enduring. My involvement in the construction of a symphony hall continues to give me as much satisfaction as anything I have ever done. Governor Rampton wrote to Senator John Warner, the national administrator of the American Revolution Bicentennial Administration:

In Utah, the achievements of the State Commission under the leadership of Obert C. Tanner have been nothing less than remarkable. Without his contribution, the Bicentennial Center for the Arts would still be a distant dream.

But, in fact, the work of many people helped Utah achieve great distinction in celebrating our country's two hundredth birthday. Our new symphony hall will greatly improve the quality of life in the third century of our great democracy.

Bicentennial of the United States Constitution

One day the telephone operator told my secretary the White House was calling. I thought it was somebody's joke. But when I answered, a woman said: "President Reagan would like to appoint you to the federal commission for the celebration of the bicentennial of the U.S. Constitution. You have been recommended by Chief Justice Warren E. Burger." I must have paused, no doubt in surprise, longer than necessary, and she repeated what she had said.

My reply was short: "Tell President Reagan I accept and that I will do my best." She cautioned: "Oh, you haven't been appointed yet. We will send you some forms to fill out and they must be approved before you are appointed." In a few days I received the forms containing a great many questions such as:

- Did I have any actual or pending lawsuits?
- Had I ever had cases in court, if so what?
- Had I ever been convicted of a crime more serious than a traffic ticket?
- If I had been cited for a traffic violation, was the fine more than thirty dollars?

After finishing several pages of questions, most all of which I answered in the negative, I said to my secretary: "I must have lived a dull life."

I went to Washington to meet with Chief Justice Burger, chairman of the commission, and with the other twenty-one members. The commission was sworn into office by Vice-President George Bush on July 30, 1985. Commission meetings were held monthly at first, then less often. Our appointment expired at the end of 1991, the bicentennial year of the ratification of the Bill of Rights.

Chief Justice Burger and I had been friends since the time he came to Utah to help us celebrate the Bicentennial of the American Revolution. Representing the judicial branch of our government, he spoke in the Tabernacle, and his speech was widely broadcast. He has returned to Utah on several occasions, and I have been honored to be his guest in Washington. I enjoyed hosting the second meeting of the bicentennial commission on August 21–23, 1985, in Salt Lake City. Besides the commission members, including Herbert Brownell, former U.S. Attorney General who became a particular friend, many federal and state executives, and an array of security people gathered at our river home for dinner one evening—an occasion I will always remember.

The purpose of the commission was to educate as many Americans as possible about the meaning of our constitution. Our chairman, called this bicentennial "a history and civics lesson" for all of us. We had an office in Washington, D.C., and over a hundred staff members dealt with the many questions and requests for help made by schools, churches, civic groups, businesses, and countless other organizations.

During my several visits to the capital city, I observed how our government works, in particular I noted the strong convictions of people involved in politics. Every individual's view on almost any subject seemed influenced by its political implications. The daily atmosphere of Washington has little to do with objectivity as it is defined in universities. Every comment, every project, in fact just about everything that happens, is weighed in terms of whether it is favorable or unfavorable to those in power or to those who would like to be in power. Our commission, though non-partisan, was composed of people who naturally held rather definite political opinions. We did experience a little of what is called "gridlock," which makes progress difficult. But I believe we did our job well.

There is an Eastern saying that fascinates me: Within limits, infinite freedom. I am sure only God's freedom is infinite, but in any human society, there must be limits to allow and protect whatever freedom there is. That is what our constitution does superbly well.

Fountains

I did not intend to become known as one who builds fountains, though that is what seems to have happened. The reasons for my love of fountains are not complex or obscure— quite the reverse. Fountains are universally pleasing. The sight and sound of running water both awakens and answers so many human moods, from carefree joy and playfulness to serenity and peace of mind. Fountains are a lovely addition to a variety of spaces—college campuses and hospitals, parks and other public institutions, and even the workplace. The design of fountains has always caught my imagination. Each fountain has its own quality of beauty, and its own story. I will mention just a few.

LDS Church Office Building Fountain

My favorite fountain is the one located in front of the high-rise office building of the Church of Jesus Christ of Latter-day Saints. It took five years to complete.

In 1970, at the close of a meeting concerned with the White House Conference on Children and Families, I mentioned to the First Presidency of the LDS church a hope I had long cherished, namely, to make a gift of a beautiful fountain on Temple Square. President Tanner asked if I would consider funding a fountain to be located in front of the nearly completed church office building. My reply was negative because of my preference for the location on Temple Square. My grandfather, Ezra T. Clark, did much to help build that beautiful temple and Grace and I had been married there.

A week later President Tanner asked if I would reconsider my decision about the location of a fountain. He explained that adequate space on Temple Square could be made, but it would be difficult. (I am glad to report that the church has since built a beautiful fountain on the square.)

This time I replied positively. He asked me to join with him as we looked over the space between Main and State streets. In a moment of fantasy, I imagined that not since the days of Brigham Young had there been such an opportunity to achieve something beautiful for the city of Salt Lake. For years to come, millions of visitors would enjoy this large central plaza. Today this space has one large fountain and four smaller ones. There are several running streams of water and the landscaping is surpassingly beautiful.

If possible, I wanted a design that would express, in a symbolic way, the distinctive spiritual values of the Mormon religion. Such a goal was not easy to acheive. How does one express intangible ideals in a visible way? In planning this new plaza, some architects were attracted to still pools of water that would reflect the temple spires. They cited persuasively the transcendent beauty of the reflection pools in front of the great Taj Mahal. But that comparison was flawed: the idea implied was not Mormon, it was Islamic. The Taj Mahal pools express the eternal and unchanging, the serene and final will of Allah in all things. Such a philosophy gives peace of mind to those who believe that "God will have it so," but that is not the dynamic of the Mormon religion. Mormons believe that human beings and God are partners. If something can be done to improve and overcome whatever impedes human joy and happiness, it should be done. Water moves and thereby can express change and progress. Accordingly, I designed a fountain where the jets would run a cycle from one small jet to larger ones, so that as it played, the fountain would become more complete, more whole, more perfect, and more beautiful, thus portraying the Mormon ideals of growth, participation, activity, and progress and, evoking that favorite doctrinal point of mine, the law of eternal progression.

The fountain was finally completed and dedicated on April 1, 1975. I have received many letters of appreciation, but one that has great meaning for me is the following:

> April 11, 1975
>
> Dear Brother Tanner:
>
> Now that the water complex on the Church Plaza has been completed and dedicated, we wish to extend to you our sincere appreciation for the contribution of your means and services in preparing the plans for this beautiful facility. Knowing you as we do, we realize that the mere fact thousands of people will enjoy this beautiful display over the years is reward enough to you. It is faith promoting to observe the conduct of public-spirited men like you who, after having made their economic future secure, are anxious to engage in worthwhile civic and philanthropic activities designed to bless their fellowmen.
>
> May the Lord continue to bless you.
>
> Sincerely yours,
> Spencer W. Kimball
> N. Eldon Tanner
> M. G. Romney
> The First Presidency

Seven Canyons Fountain

Recently the Seven Canyons Fountain at Liberty Park was dedicated by Deedee Corradini, mayor of Salt Lake. It was a pleasant day for Grace, our friends, and a few distinguished citizens. On June 17, 1993, the *Salt Lake Tribune* wrote an editorial entitled "Obert's Fountains":

> There's something mystical, something soothing about water playing over rocks in the sunlight—a gurgling brook, a flowing fountain, a gentle rain. And, of course, because of its rarity, there's nothing like water dancing in the desert.
>
> The new Seven Canyons fountain at Liberty Park may be one of the most impressive projects Mr. Tanner has inspired. This 30,000-square-foot creation is intended as a miniature of the canyons of the Wasatch Mountains in Salt Lake County, and it evokes what Wordsworth might have described when he wrote of "waters, rolling from their moun-tainsprings, with a soft inland murmur."
>
> Poets, prophets and philosophers have understood the restorative powers of flowing water from the beginning of time, and so, apparently, does Mr. Tanner. That he has chosen to share this gift with countless people in Utah and elsewhere speaks of a man attuned to life's beauty and one of its more congenial mysteries.

Hospital Fountains

A fountain is a lovely entrance to a hospital, symbolizing all the joys and sorrows that bring people there. At the dedication of the fountain at St. Mark's Hospital, I mentioned a wide range of human emotions:

A hospital is a place where the unforgettable events in human life take place. Some events are glad, some sad, and always there is tension and worry and deep concern for those who come to a hospital in need of help. A fountain, in its way, speaks to these various moods and moments of crisis.

Clear and tumbling waters seem to share joy and gladness when a baby is born. And when deep sorrow comes, a fountain seems to give a small measure of serenity to the human spirit. The crisis of tragedy seeks and hopes for some reconciliation, some larger understanding. A hospital will always be a place of concern, of tension, of anxiety. But a fountain may help, if only so slightly, to lift the human spirit, and help give some peace of mind to those who pause here.

On May 17, 1990, the Primary Children's Hospital was dedicated. The fountain there is of large dolomite granite boulders brought from Wisconsin. The design was created by the architects of the beautiful building. Children were kept in mind—in the gentle structure of rock and water, and in the quotations on the plaque there:

> *If anyone gives so much as a cup of cold water to one of these little ones, he will not lose his reward.*
> —Matthew 10:42

University Fountains

When we were planning a fountain at Stanford University, Grace and I were invited to go to the top of Hoover Tower and look over possible locations. I favored the open oval space at the end of Palm Drive, but Stanford's architect opposed this location. Then, because Herbert Hoover was a hero of mine, I thought it would be nice to have a fountain in front of the building named for him. When it was completed, the university placed a small plaque in memory of our oldest son, Dean.

Perhaps the most unusual fountain, if not the most spectacular, is the one at Harvard University. President Derek C. Bok and I were once chatting when he was in Salt Lake for a session of the trustees of the Tanner Lectures. He asked about my interest in fountains and I replied, "Yes, in designing and building fountains, I've made every mistake there is." He was intrigued, and soon I was on my way to Cambridge with my architect, Boyd Blackner, who has helped me design many fountains. I had spent two years there in graduate work, and I wanted Harvard to have a truly beautiful fountain.

The result is a circular area of large rocks or boulders brought in from western Massachusetts. Jets spray a mist over the area and rainbows form here and there as light is refracted through the mist. Surrounded by green lawns and trees, the setting has become a popular place for students to pause briefly and relax during their busy schedules. Frequently observers of the fountain write to tell me of children playing there. It pleased Derek Bok to let me know that in 1985 our fountain, designed by Peter Walker, received a prestigious award from the Boston Society of Landscape Architects. In an article in the *Boston Globe,* September 10, 1992, Boston is described as a "city of fountains":

> Across the river, as we make our way through Cambridge, there are several small scale but memorable water sculptures. Our favorite is Tanner Fountain outside the Harvard Science Center between the yard, Memorial Hall and that stretch of looming red Victorian buildings on Oxford Street.
>
> Were it not for Tanner Fountain, the confluence of this tight, close, heat retaining Victoriana

might cause summer madness. But instead, joining these diverse architectural expressions, is a pastoral spread of fieldstone, field and mist. Specifically, a landscaped grassy area with scores of jagged, homey, boulders surrounds a fountain that emits spray so fine it's seen as a haze or mist.

. . . It has a Stonehenge-like friendliness and monumentality. Passersby are drawn to the fountain; those who live in the neighborhood make ridiculous detours to walk by it. In the darkness of evening, we occasionally lose all dignity, surrender to its spell and walk through the configuration of rocks into the mist. If only there were fireflies . . .

The waters of the fountain constructed on the plaza east of the Marriott Library at the University of Utah tumble over a complex series of concrete cubes to create the effect of a canyon stream. My first visit to this fountain was on a hot summer day. Children and students were wading in the pool and along the concrete slabs at the sides. As I stood there I was disturbed by what I considered might become a health risk, such as a swimming pool may create. But as I listened to their laughter and happy voices, I realized this was why fountains are built, to provide joy and relaxation. After a few minutes I removed my own shoes, rolled up my trousers, and joined the group. It was an exhilarating experience.

A Famous Lectureship

I have enjoyed endowing lectures at various universities. For me a lecture is a symbol of university life, a microcosm of its larger mission—the sharing of knowledge. The most ambitious and well-known of these lecture series is the Tanner Lectures on Human Values. They started modestly enough. In 1975, Dixie College dedicated a fountain. The speaker on that occasion was Sterling McMurrin, and as we walked from the college to our motel, Sterling said, "Obert, I think I know a better way to spend your money." He suggested a lectureship. In that beginning our thought was about a single lecture at the University of Utah. But this idea expanded in time.

Today the Tanner Lectures on Human Values are given annually at nine of the world's great universities: University of California; Clare Hall, Cambridge University, England; Harvard University; University of Michigan; Brasenose College, Oxford University, England; Princeton University; Stanford University; University of Utah; and Yale University. Each institution selects its own lecturer from among the world's outstanding scholars, artists, and political leaders. The lectures are published annually, in a single volume, and made available to libraries throughout the world.

Perhaps the single most important factor in the success of these lectures has been the personal involvement of the university presidents. All nine presidents with their spouses, and other trustees, gather each year during the last week of June, to discuss the experiences of each lecture during the past year, and to make plans for the future. Our work is done with ease and enjoyment, and a great sense of friendship has developed over the years. No doubt these leaders have similar challenges and satisfactions in their work, and they enjoy sharing their experiences and learning from each other.

I recall our first meeting at Cambridge University where the lectureship was established in 1978. I thought I was prepared for the occasion, but I found it quite overwhelming to sit with these world leaders in education. When it came my turn I said, "Some of you may say you have never met a perfectly happy man. Now you will not be able to say that again." And, to a remarkable extent, my happiness persists to this day.

The Tanner Lectures on Human Values attract the world's ablest minds, not only from university faculties, but from among distinguished leaders in the world of practical affairs. The annual publication of the lectures adds knowledge that can make a difference in the world. Volume 14 has just been published. Having spent so much of my own life in universities—both as student and teacher—I feel a great satisfaction in giving back some of what I have gained, through these and other lectures, as well as furnishing library rooms, building fountains, and helping with publications and scholarships.

Theatres

Under the supervision of Fred Adams, Grace's cousin, a great Shakespearean Festival is held each year at Southern Utah University. Grace is an alumna of that college (now a university), which is not far from her childhood home in Parowan, and so annually we have loved attending this world-famous festival. Once Shakespeare was played there on a small stage with temporary seats. Now it is played in what the Folger Library has described as the best existing replica of a Tudor playhouse. It is a gift in honor of Grace and her parents.

Grace's "Uncle Will L." produced plays for many years in southern Utah, with Grace playing leading roles during her high school and college days. Her cousin, Fred, is something of a genius in his production of plays by Shakespeare. Some measure of talent must run in the Adams family.

At Springdale, near the entrance to Zion National Park, is a splendid outdoor amphitheatre we worked six years to help build. It is situated beneath a rock formation called the Three Marys. In the evening, when lights are turned on, beautiful Zion Park is seen in all its majesty. Plays and performances of various kinds are presented in this setting. Each summer the Utah Symphony gives a concert there.

Grace has also enjoyed helping with Red Butte Garden, a botanical garden near the University of Utah. For many years she supported the research of Walter P. Cottam, renowned University of Utah botanist. On July 18, 1992, President George Bush made a visit to Utah, and gave his address on the environment in the amphitheatre at Red Butte. An annual Greek theatrical festival is performed there, as well as a summer concert series.

A Rose Garden

A beautiful rose garden at the Holy Cross Hospital had for many years been a community showplace in Salt Lake City. A number of years ago, the original rose garden had to be abandoned when the hospital was renovated. Our restoration has, therefore, been "the return of the roses." At one end of the garden, next to a large evergreen, is a beautiful madonna and child called "Madonna of the Street." It is one of the loveliest pieces of art in Utah. The rose garden has once more become a place of beauty and serenity. It was dedicated in June 1990, with the following comments:

> We have at last come to think more about the beauty of our planet-earth. In restoring this rose garden, we make our earth a little more beautiful. Even more beautiful than flowers, is the inner beauty of the Sisters of the Holy Cross who labor here.
>
> Nearby in rooms that overlook this garden, other children will yet be born to bless this planet-earth. This great hospital, now has two places, where all may go: inside, is a chalice fountain and a chapel for prayer and meditation. Outside, after many years, is the restoration of this lovely rose garden. In both, we ponder the gladness and sadness of human life, the wonder of birth and the mystery of death. In this hospital one may find relief from pain, and in this garden one may find peace of mind and a larger measure of goodwill.

We thank those who labor here. We cherish Sisters who desire to serve God by serving mankind.

Invitation to the White House

In 1988, I was invited to the White House, to receive the National Medal of Arts for my work as a patron of the arts. When my plane was slipping down over farms and houses approaching Dulles Airport, I found myself reflecting that the purpose of this occasion was not a business appointment, no bicentennial commission meetings. This time it was to receive an award presented by the President of the United States. I shall always remember those few moments of reflection before the plane landed.

The *Washington Post* reported on that occasion:

> [Mr. Tanner] talks not of billions but of beauty. "I love beauty," said the Utah businessman, retired philosophy professor and music and theatre philanthropist. Chairman of the board of a company he founded that makes what he called "employee recognition emblems," Tanner has also designed and given away . . . fountains to such institutions as Harvard, Stanford and Oxford universities.
>
> "A fountain is democratic," he said. "Everyone can enjoy it and everyone does. It's noncontroversial. I've been a critical philosopher in my time, and I've had my share of arguments and dissent, and now I kind of like something that nobody disagrees with."

At the White House luncheon, the twelve honorees were seated, six at a table hosted by Mrs. Reagan, and six with President Reagan. At the President's table were actress Helen

Hayes; architect I. M. Pei; pianist Rudolf Serkin; composer Virgil Thompson; and two art patrons, Brooks Astor and myself. President Reagan was a delightful host. He told with good humor some of his experiences in the presidency, and related a few facts from a two-volume history of the White House he was then reading. And since Congress funded the award, we were invited to join with members of the House and Senate. We met in the Mike Mansfield Room near the Senate chambers. The speakers were Senators Ted Kennedy and Alan Simpson. Altogether it was an occasion I cherish greatly. The joy of giving, and, I hope, of receiving too, will endure for a long, long time.

EPILOGUE

. . .

EPILOGUE

• • •

My life has spanned most of an amazing century, encompassing monumental events: the World Wars, the Great Depression, the Cold War, and extensive political changes that are occurring now. This century has been described as an "Age of Anxiety." It has been a century of revolutions and counterrevolutions—political, economic, and social. Many difficult problems will carry over into the coming century, including those of the environment, population growth, political instability, and economic imbalance.

As I look back over my life, I see three values at work. I did not invent them. I did not achieve them. They were recurring challenges, lights to live by, and graces to enjoy. They are known by the labels *freedom*, *kindness*, and *beauty*.

Freedom is the most familiar and continuous theme of this narrative. It was there from my early days in Farmington, Utah, and remains a major value today. I try to encourage it for others. I have stressed my belief that a good family is one in which children are encouraged to claim their freedom, and that a good society allows expansiveness, change, and variety. Entrenched powers, whether in authority roles, accepted ideologies, or institutional structures, are common and necessary to every culture, yet these powers often work against our finding the best solutions to our problems, the best answers to our questions, because they limit freedom to search.

Beauty and kindness are closer to being ends in themselves. When either of them touches our lives, we are lifted from the ordinariness of day-to-day human experience. We feel the gift of life, and the energy of love. My life has been abundantly blessed by the serenity that beauty brings, and by the grace of kindness. I hope I have passed some of that on, here and there.

The eighty-nine years I have lived are years filled with a mix of the good and the not-so-good, with gladness and sadness, hope and despair. But overall, and on the whole, I have been blessed. It has been a good life—successful even— in the sense described by Ralph Waldo Emerson:

> *Success is to laugh often and much;*
> *to win the respect of intelligent people*
> *and the affection of children;*
> *to earn the appreciation of honest critics*
> *and endure the betrayal of false friends.*
>
> *Success is to appreciate beauty,*
> *to find the best in others;*
> *to leave the world a bit better,*
> *whether by a healthy child,*
> *a garden patch,*
> *or a redeemed social condition;*
> *to know even one life has breathed easier*
> *because you lived.*

AFTERWORD

. . .

Obert C. Tanner died on October 14, 1993, still fine tuning the words of this manuscript and still on his journey in search of freedom.

APPENDIXES

∎ ∎ ∎

Appendix A

Degrees

Earned

University of Utah—Bachelor of Arts, 1929

University of Utah—Bachelor of Laws, 1936

Stanford University—Master of Arts in Philosophy, 1937

University of Utah—Juris Doctor, 1967

Honorary

Utah State University—Doctor of Humanities, 1968

Southern Utah University—Doctor of Letters, 1972

University of Utah—Doctor of Laws, 1972

Westminster College—Doctor of Letters, 1972

College of Eastern Utah—Associate Doctor's Degree, 1978

Dixie College—Associate in Arts Degree, 1980

Weber State University—Doctor of Humanities, 1985

Appendix B

Honors

Beehive Hall of Fame, 1982

Brigham Young University—Presidential Citation, 1991

Cambridge University—Honorary Fellowship of Clare Hall, 1987

Manufacturing Jewelers and Silversmiths of America—Hall of Fame, 1992

National Conference of Christians and Jews—Brotherhood Award, 1971

National Medal of Arts, presented by the President of the United States, 1988

Newcomen Society of North America—Obert C. Tanner and the Tanner Company, 1981

Oxford University—Honorary Fellowship of Linacre College, 1988

United Nations Association/United States of America—Peace Medal, 1978

Phi Beta Kappa Honorary, 1977

Phi Delta Kappa—Distinguished Service to Education, 1984

Phi Kappa Phi Honorary, 1969

The American Society of the Most Venerable Order of the Hospital of St. John of Jerusalem, 1980; Grade of Knight, 1989

University of Utah—Beehive Honor Society, 1979

University of Utah—Professor Emeritus of Philosophy, 1974

Utah Business Hall of Fame, 1991

Utah Governor's Award for the Arts, 1981

Appendix C

Published Works

New Testament Outlines. Seminary manual. Church of Jesus Christ of Latter-day Saints. 1927. Reprinted.

Problems of Youth. Co-author, Adam S. Bennion. Written for LDS Junior Seminaries. Department of Education. Church of Jesus Christ of Latter-day Saints. 1931. Reprinted.

Looking in on Greatness. Co-author, Adam S. Bennion. Written for LDS Junior Seminaries. Department of Education. Church of Jesus Christ of Latter-day Saints. 1932. Reprinted.

New Testament Studies. Department of Education. Church of Jesus Christ of Latter-day Saints. 1932. Reprinted.

The New Testament Speaks. Department of Education. Church of Jesus Christ of Latter-day Saints. 1935. Reprinted.

Stanford Memorial Church. Stanford University Press. 1946.

Christ's Ideals for Living. Sunday School manual. Church of Jesus Christ of Latter-day Saints. 1955.

Bicentennial Center for the Arts. Report of Utah's Bicentennial Celebration of the American Revolution. 1978.

One Man's Search: Addresses by Obert C. Tanner. University of Utah Press. 1989.

Toward Understanding the New Testament. Co-authors, Lewis M. Rogers and Sterling M. McMurrin. Signature Books. 1990.

One Man's Journey in Search of Freedom. The Humanities Center at the University of Utah. 1994.

Appendix D

Endowed Lectures

Tanner Lectures on Human Values

University of California

Clare Hall, Cambridge University, England

Harvard University

University of Michigan

Brasenose College, Oxford University, England

Princeton University

Stanford University

University of Utah

Yale University

Ashby Lecture

Clare Hall, Cambridge University, England

The Juanita Brooks Western History and Culture Lecture

Dixie College

The Sissela Bok Lectures on Moral Philosophy

Harvard University

The David Pierpont Gardner Graduate Lecture in the Humanities and Fine Arts

University of Utah

The Hart Lecture on Jurisprudence and Moral Philosophy

Oxford University

The Sterling M. McMurrin Distinguished Visiting Professorship Lectures

University of Utah

The Mormon History Association Tanner Lecture

The Annie Clark Tanner Lectureship on Family Development

Weber State College

The Grace A. Tanner Lecture on Human Values

Snow College

Appendixes

The Grace Adams Tanner Lectures on Human Values

Southern Utah University

The Joseph Marion Tanner Lecture on Moral Philosophy

Utah State University

The O. C. Tanner Academy Lecture

Utah Academy of Sciences, Arts, and Letters

The Tanner-McMurrin Lectures on the Philosophy and History of Religion

Westminster College

The O. Meredith Wilson Lecture in History

University of Utah

Myron Tanner Lecture

Brigham Young University

John Tanner Lecture

Brigham Young University

Appendix E

Special Rooms and Libraries

Brigham Young University, David O. McKay and Adam S. Bennion Library Reception Room

Brigham Young University, Tanner Memorial Philosophy Library Collection

Harvard University, Emerson Hall, Faculty Seminar Room and Philosophy Department offices

Harvard University, Emerson Hall, Mrs. C. I. Lewis Philosophy Periodical Reading Room

University of Michigan, Angel Hall, Philosophy Reading Room and Library

Oxford University, Linacre College, Tanner Library

Southern Utah University, Founders Room, Randall Jones Memorial Theatre

Southern Utah University, Grace A. Tanner Library Center for Human Values

Stanford University, Tanner Memorial Philosophy Library

University of Utah, Alumni House, Grace Tanner Dining Room

University of Utah, College of Law Faculty Room

University of Utah, Annie Clark Tanner Library Room

University of Utah, Tanner Room, Philosophy Department

Utah State University, College of Business, Faculty and Graduate Student Reading Room

Utah State University, J. M. Tanner Library Reading Room

Utah Symphony Hall, Maestro and Musicians' Rooms

Appendix F

Funded Publications

A Mormon Mother: An Autobiography. Annie Clark Tanner. 1973.

Letters of Long Ago. Agnes Just Reid, edited by Brigham D. Madsen. 1973.

"Dear Ellen," Two Mormon Women and Their Letters. Edited by S. George Ellsworth. 1974.

Twelve Mormon Homes Visited in Succession on a Journey Through Utah to Arizona. Elizabeth Wood Kane, edited by Everett L. Cooley. 1974.

A Biography of Ezra Thompson Clark. Annie Clark Tanner. 1975.

An Army Wife on the Frontier: The Memoirs of Alice Blackwood Baldwin, 1867-77. Edited by Robert C. and Eleanor R. Carriker. 1975.

A Governor's Wife on the Mining Frontier: The Letters of Mary Edgerton from Montana, 1863-65. Edited by James L. Thane, Jr. 1976.

The Genteel Gentile: Letters of Elizabeth Cumming, 1857-58. Edited by Ray R. Canning and Beverly Beeton. 1977.

Diary of Brigham Young. Edited by Everett L. Cooley. 1980.

A Fragment: The Autobiography of Mary Jane Mount Tanner. Edited by Margery W. Ward. 1980.

A Forty-niner in Utah with the Stansbury Exploration of Great Salt Lake: Letters and Journal of John Hudson, 1848-50. Edited by Brigham D. Madsen. 1981

A Basket of Chips: An Autobiography by James Taylor Harwood. Edited by Robert S. Olpin. 1985.

The Restored Gospel and Applied Christianity: Student Essays in Honor of President David O. McKay. Annual David O. McKay Essay Contest. Brigham Young University.

Appendix G

Fountains

Water and meditation are wedded forever

—Melville

Alta View Hospital, Sandy, Utah, 1986

Brigham Young University, N. Eldon Tanner building atrium, Provo, Utah, 1981

Brigham Young University, Provo, Utah, 1985

Church of Jesus Christ of Latter-day Saints Plaza, Salt Lake City, Utah, 1975

City of Orem, Utah, 1987

City of Parowan, Utah, Heritage Park, 1993

College of Eastern Utah, Price, 1981

Cottonwood Hospital, Murray, Utah, 1984

Dixie College, St. George, Utah, 1975

Hansen Planetarium, Salt Lake City, Utah, 1975

Harvard University, Cambridge, Massachusetts, 1985

Holy Cross Hospital/Jordan Valley, Utah, 1983

Holy Cross Hospital/Jordan Valley, Utah, Chalice Fountain, 1993

Holy Cross Hospital/Salt Lake City, Utah, Chalice Fountain, 1988

Holy Cross Hospital/Salt Lake City, Utah, Rose Garden Fountain, 1990

LDS Hospital, Salt Lake City, Utah, 1985

Liberty Park, Seven-Canyon Fountain, Salt Lake City, Utah, 1993

Logan City, Utah, 1990

Oxford University, Linacre College, England, 1987

Primary Children's Medical Center, Salt Lake City, Utah, 1990

Salt Lake Community College, Utah, 1985

Sevier Valley Technical College, Richfield, Utah, 1980

Snow College, Ephraim, Utah, 1978

Southern Utah University, Cedar City, 1982

Spanish Fork, Utah, Memorial Park, 1990

St. George, Utah, Civic Center, 1988

St. Mark's Hospital, Salt Lake City, Utah, 1976

Stanford University, Palo Alto, California, 1978

Symphony Hall, Salt Lake City, Utah, 1979

O. C. Tanner Company fountains (8)

Tanner Park, Salt Lake City, Utah, 1982

Uintah Basin Area Vocational Center, Roosevelt, Utah, 1980

University of Utah, Library Plaza, Salt Lake City, 1970

University of Utah, Obert C. Tanner Plaza, Salt Lake City, 1986

University of Utah Medical Center, Salt Lake City, 1990

Utah Community Center for the Deaf, Salt Lake City, 1992

Utah State University, Obert C. Tanner Fountain and Plaza, 1980

Utah Valley Community College, Orem, 1982

Utah Valley Regional Medical Center, Provo, 1986

Westminster College, Salt Lake City, Utah, 1971

Whitmore Library, Salt Lake City, Utah, 1980

Appendix H

Tanner Family

Children of Annie Clark (1864-1941) *and Joseph Marion Tanner* (1859-1927)

Jennie Tanner Fairbanks (1888-1923)

Myron Clark Tanner (1890-1958)

Herschel Clark Tanner (1893-1968)

LaVinz Clark Tanner (1895-1973)

Belva Tanner (1897-1897)

Kneland Clark Tanner (1898-1968)

Sheldon Clark Tanner (1900-1966)

Lois Tanner Morrill Robertson (1902-1974)

Leah Tanner (1902-1905)

Obert Clark Tanner (1904-1993)

Children of Grace Adams and Obert C. Tanner

Dean Obert Tanner (1933-1943)

Joan Tanner Reddish (1936-)

Gordon Adams Tanner (1938-1955)

Carolyn Tanner Irish (1940-)

Stephen Clark Tanner (1943-1949)

David Obert Tanner (1951-)

Photographic Credits

All photographs reproduced in this book came from the Tanner family collection or the archives of the O.C. Tanner Company. In many cases, the name of the original photographer has been lost. Additional credits are given below.

Page 77: photograph of J. M. Tanner courtesy of Glenbow Archives, Calgary, Alberta, Canada.

Page 142: photograph of Tanner Fountain at Harvard University courtesy of Jim Harrison (Charlestown, Massachusetts) and Zona Photographic Laboratories.

Page 143: photograph of Tanner Fountain at Stanford University courtesy of Arthur Streiber © 1985.

Page 146: photograph of first Tanner Company building on South State Street by Hal Rumel; photograph of current Tanner Company headquarters by Michael Schoenfeld.

INDEX

. . .

Index

Wixom, Jack, 5
Wood, J. D., 32, 67
Wright, Carol Adams, 95
Wright, William, 95

Yale University, lecture, 210

Zion National Park, amphitheatre,
   211